Shattered Reflections:
Unraveling the Hidden Journey of Black Male Student Success

Dr. Samuel Essah-Hienwo

TABLE OF CONTENTS

Introduction

Amidst the whispers of history, an echo grows louder—a tale of resilience tangled with silent battles. Can you hear it? The year is 1954, and the Supreme Court declares "separate but equal" unconstitutional. A seismic shift, yet the tremors of change move slowly. It's a time of great promise, but promises are not self-fulfilling. Decades since then, a paradox unfolds; doors of opportunity creak open while invisible barriers stand resilient. Why, then, does the reflection of black male success remain fragmented in the halls of academia? Their journey—a labyrinth of systemic challenges, punctuated by the haunting absence of paternal figures. Pause and ponder. What happens to potential when it echoes in a void of guidance? Each page turned in this book is a step closer to unraveling that mystery. But as we venture deeper into these hidden corridors, be warned—the truths we uncover may shatter reflections we once thought whole. And just when the pieces begin to align...

CHAPTER 1
The Shadow of Absence

DEFINING PATERNAL ABSENCE

In the intricate tapestry of academic success, threads of various hues and textures intertwine, creating patterns that tell stories of triumph and tribulation alike. Yet, amidst this rich mosaic, certain threads run faint, their absence casting shadows on the overall picture. Such is the subtle yet profound impact of paternal absence in the lives of black male students, a gap that reverberates through their academic journey. To fully grasp this phenomenon, one must first dissect the language that forms the backbone of our understanding.

Engaging with the nuanced landscape of paternal absence requires the illumination of keywords that serve as beacons, guiding us through the murky waters of this complex issue. These terms—paternal, absence, academic success, and black male students—are not merely words but represent vast concepts with deep-seated implications.

Paternal, derived from the Latin 'pater' meaning father, refers to that which relates to a father or fatherhood. In the context of our exploration, it extends beyond the mere biological connection to encompass the emotional, psychological, and sociocultural roles that fathers or father figures traditionally fulfill.

Absence, on the other hand, connotes more than the physical nonexistence of a person. It encapsulates the lack of emotional support, guidance, and engagement that are essential for the holistic development of a child. When juxtaposed with paternal, the term paternal absence emerges as a void, a chasm left by a father's lack of presence.

The term academic success is not confined to the attainment of high grades or the accumulation of accolades. It embodies the full spectrum of educational achievements, including the development of critical thinking, the pursuit of knowledge, and the cultivation of skills necessary for personal growth and societal contribution.

Black male students, the focal point of this discourse, are individuals who carry with them the weight of history and the aspirations of a community. They navigate an educational landscape that is often uneven, their paths strewn with obstacles that are both visible and invisible.

Let's delve further into these terms, unraveling the threads to understand how they weave into the lives of these students. The absence of a father—or a paternal figure—can transform the educational odyssey into a solo expedition fraught with uncertainties. Without the compass of paternal guidance, black male students may struggle to find the true north of their potential.

Imagine a garden where the gardener's presence is vital for the nurturing of young saplings. The gardener's touch, his knowledge of the soil, and his understanding of the elements all contribute to the growth of sturdy, vibrant plants. Now, picture that garden untended, the absence of the gardener's wisdom and care leading to an unpredictable outcome. This garden is a familiar concept that echoes the role of a father figure in the developmental garden of a child's life.

Yet, the absence of a paternal figure does not seal one's fate. It is not an unchangeable verdict but a challenge that, when recognized, can be met with resilience and innovation. There are countless stories of black male students who, despite the void left by paternal absence, have forged paths of success with the tools of determination, community support, and self-belief.

What happens, then, when one must navigate the academic terrain without a paternal guide? How does one cultivate resilience in the harsh soil of absence? It is within the answers to these questions that we find the strength and adaptability of the human spirit.

The exploration of paternal absence is not complete without acknowledging the myriad ways in which black male students have compensated for this gap. Mentorship programs, peer networks, and the indomitable will of mothers and other family members often step in to fill the void. They become the architects of success, constructing scaffolds of support upon which these students can ascend.

In the silent halls of academia, where black male students walk, the echoes of paternal absence reverberate. But with each step, they are also crafting new reflections, piecing together shards of determination, hope, and achievement. Their journey is a testament to the power of the human spirit to transcend absence and to the undying belief that success is not a gift bestowed by circumstance but a crown forged in the fires of perseverance.

In this chapter, we have not merely defined terms; we have peeled back layers, exposing the roots that anchor the complex reality of black male students' quest for academic success. It is a narrative punctuated by the absence of paternal figures, yet it is also a narrative of unwavering strength and endless possibility.

As we close this section of their story, we must remember that the journey does not end here. The reflections may be shattered, but the pieces are in our hands, ready to be assembled into a mosaic of understanding and insight. The path ahead is one of continued exploration and unwavering commitment to illuminating the hidden journey of black male student success.

Psychological Impacts

In the quiet afterglow of understanding the linguistic underpinnings of paternal absence, one must now venture into the labyrinth of the human psyche, exploring the psychological impacts that such a void can have on black male students. These young men venture into the world with a blueprint that often lacks the foundational support of a father figure, a deficit that can ripple through their mental and emotional landscapes with profound consequences.

The current issue at hand lies not just in the physical absence of a father but in the missing emotional scaffolding that a father figure can provide. A father or father figure often stands as a pillar of strength, discipline, and emotional support. In the lives of young black men, this pillar, when absent, leaves a space where doubts and insecurities may flourish unchecked.

The consequences of such an absence are manifold and deeply entrenched. It can lead to an identity crisis, where these individuals grapple with their sense of self and their role within the community and the broader society. They may experience heightened levels of anxiety and depression stemming from the unresolved emotional turmoil and the pressure to navigate a world that demands resilience in the face of stark social and economic challenges.

What could happen if this issue remains unaddressed? The landscape of these young men's futures may become overgrown with the brambles of unfulfilled potential and the thorns of societal disenfranchisement. Mental health struggles could escalate, leading to a higher risk of engaging in detrimental behaviors, and a chasm between their lived experiences and the opportunities afforded to their peers may widen.

But what if there was a way to bridge this gap, to provide the support and guidance that a father figure embodies? Herein lies a solution steeped in communal strength and collective wisdom. Mentorship programs tailored to the needs of black male students could serve as the cornerstone of this support system, offering a surrogate for the lost paternal presence.

To implement such a solution, communities and educational institutions must collaborate to create networks of positive male role models. These mentors would not only offer guidance and support but also serve as tangible representations of success and perseverance. They would be the mirrors in which these young men could see the reflections of their potential.

How do we know that mentorship can be effective? Consider the projected outcomes: a mentor can provide a young man with a sense of stability and continuity, reducing feelings of isolation and abandonment. Such relationships have been shown to improve academic performance, enhance self-esteem, and foster a sense of belonging—key factors in the emotional well-being and success of black male students.

While mentorship stands as a promising solution, it is not the only one. Alternative strategies may include creating stronger community support networks, implementing fatherhood programs that encourage the involvement of absent fathers, and providing access to mental health services that are culturally sensitive and readily available.

The tapestry of solutions is rich and varied, each thread woven with the intent of mending the shattered reflections these young men face. It is in the careful crafting of these solutions that the hidden journey of black male student success can be illuminated and transformed into a pathway paved with hope and opportunity.

The psychological impacts of growing up without a father figure are not indelible scars but challenges that call for a concerted and compassionate response. Through mentorship, community support, and a commitment to addressing mental health needs, we can begin to reconstruct the broken images into a portrait of strength, resilience, and triumph. The journey is undoubtedly arduous, but the destination—a future where every black male student can look into the mirror and see a reflection whole and unbroken—is a vision worth striving for.

Social Expectations and Stereotypes

As the dawn stretches its fingers across the horizon, casting a warm glow on the university campus, the day promises new challenges and triumphs for the young men navigating the collegiate landscape. This is a place of higher learning, where the bricks and ivy are not just architectural adornments but symbols of academic aspirations. Yet, within these hallowed halls, black male students carry an additional burden, a weight forged by the societal expectations and stereotypes that shape their daily experiences.

We meet Marcus, a sophomore majoring in engineering whose intelligence and drive are often overshadowed by the preconceived notions held by others. He is a diligent student, but his demeanor is occasionally misread as unapproachable, his assertiveness as aggression. Alongside him is Elijah, a freshman athlete whose prowess on the basketball court is celebrated, yet his academic ambitions are frequently underestimated. These young men are the main players in our story, emblematic of the broader population of black male students striving against a current of bias and misconception.

The challenge they face is multifaceted: it is the struggle to disprove the stereotypes that cast them as less capable, less scholarly, and more prone to disciplinary issues. It is the constant pressure to perform not only for personal success but to counteract the narratives that society has written for them. The problem is pervasive, affecting their academic performance, mental health, and future trajectories.

Marcus, Elijah, and their peers adopt a variety of strategies to navigate these societal expectations. They form study groups to bolster academic success, engage in campus organizations to build leadership skills and seek mentors who can provide guidance and support. They also challenge the stereotypes through their actions, proving their detractors wrong by excelling in their studies and contributing positively to the campus community.

The results of these strategies are promising. Marcus secures an internship with a leading tech company, breaking through barriers and affirming his professional capabilities. Elijah maintains a strong GPA, dispelling the myth that his athletic commitments come at the expense of his intellectual growth. These victories, however, are not just personal; they represent a larger shift in the narrative around black male student success.

Reflecting on these case studies, we recognize that while individual efforts are critical, systemic change is imperative. The stereotypes harbored within academic institutions and society at large must be dismantled. This requires ongoing dialogue, education, and policy reforms to create environments where black male students are seen for their potential, not prejudged by their skin color.

Visual aids, such as infographics displaying the achievements of black male students, can offer powerful counterpoints to prevailing stereotypes. They not only highlight success stories but also serve as inspirational tools for other students facing similar challenges.

Connecting these individual stories to the larger narrative, it becomes clear that the success of black male students is not an isolated concern but a societal imperative. Their triumphs are a testament to the resilience and tenacity inherent in the human spirit, challenging us to confront and transform the biases that limit potential.

What if society chose to see Marcus, Elijah, and countless others like them not as stereotypes but as individuals with unique talents and aspirations? What further successes might we witness, and how would our perception of black male students potential change?

As we close this chapter, let the lingering thought be one of introspection: How can each of us contribute to reshaping the narrative, fostering an environment where every student has the opportunity to shatter the distorted reflections of societal expectations and stereotypes? For it is in the collective effort to embrace diversity and inclusivity that we pave the way for a future rich with promise and unbounded by prejudice.

ACADEMIC PERFORMANCE CORRELATIONS

The stillness of the library is palpable, a sanctuary where the echoes of ambition and perseverance resonate through the rows of books. Within this quietude, young men like Marcus and Elijah seek knowledge, their eyes scanning texts not merely for information but for the keys to unlock their future. However, the path to academic success for these scholars is often entwined with the specter of fatherlessness—an absence that reverberates through their lives and educational journeys.

The stark correlation between fatherlessness and educational outcomes is a pervasive issue that demands scrutiny. Studies have consistently shown that children raised in father-absent homes are more likely to drop out of school and face disciplinary problems. Yet, this claim warrants a deeper examination beyond the surface statistics, delving into the lived experiences of those it affects.

Father absence is a multifaceted phenomenon that can result from various circumstances, including divorce, incarceration, or death. Its impact on educational achievement is profound, often setting into motion a cascade of challenges. Primary evidence of this claim can be found in the analysis of academic performance metrics. Data from the National Center for Education Statistics indicates that children from single-parent families generally score lower on standardized tests and have lower graduation rates.

But what does this mean for our young men like Marcus and Elijah? The absence of a father figure can lead to a lack of male role models, which is critical in shaping a boy's understanding of responsibility, work ethic, and personal development. This void can manifest in classroom behavior, motivation, and, ultimately, academic performance.

Yet, to delve deeper into this evidence is to recognize the resilience and potential for compensatory mechanisms within these young men's lives. Mentors, teachers, and community leaders often step into the role of the absent father, providing guidance and support. Moreover, initiatives that focus on fostering leadership skills and academic excellence can mitigate the negative impacts of fatherlessness. Programs like mentorship and tutoring have been shown to improve academic outcomes, offering a supportive scaffold where familial structures may falter.

However, there exist counter-evidence and counterarguments that challenge the initial claim, suggesting that fatherlessness is not a definitive predictor of poor educational outcomes. Some argue that economic factors, more than family structure, are the primary determinants of a student's academic success. Additionally, examples of individuals who have thrived in spite of growing up without a father figure serve to challenge the narrative that fatherlessness is an insurmountable obstacle.

In response, it is crucial to provide a rebuttal or clarification that acknowledges the complexity of the issue. While economic stability is indeed a significant factor, the role of an involved father or father figure cannot be dismissed. The nuances of individual experiences mean that while fatherlessness may not be the sole determinant of academic performance, it is a contributing factor that intersects with other social and economic variables.

To reinforce this point, additional supporting evidence can be drawn from psychological studies that emphasize the importance of father engagement in cognitive development and emotional well-being. Fathers who are actively involved in their children's education contribute to a more positive academic self-concept, which is linked to higher achievement.

In conclusion, the assertion that fatherlessness is linked to less favorable educational outcomes holds weight, yet it is not the entire story. The journey of black male student success is a tapestry woven with threads of challenge, resilience, and the power of supportive relationships. By understanding and addressing the complex factors that contribute to academic achievement, including the role of father figures, we can better support students like Marcus and Elijah in their pursuit of excellence.

As we ponder the narratives of these young men, we are left to consider the broader implications of our findings. What societal changes are necessary to support the success of students growing up without fathers? How can we, as a community, step in to fill the gaps left by absence? The answers to these questions are crucial in shaping a future where every student has the opportunity to reflect not a shattered image but a complete and empowered self.

NARRATIVES OF RESILIENCE

The sun was just beginning to dip below the horizon, casting a golden glow over the bustling campus. Among the throngs of students, there was Jordan, whose brisk stride and focused gaze set him apart. His backpack, heavy with books, was a testament to his relentless pursuit of knowledge—a pursuit he undertook without a father's guidance.

Jordan's story was not uncommon. Like many of his peers, he was navigating the academic rigors of university life without the roadmap that a paternal figure might provide. Yet, as I began to peel back the layers of his journey, what became evident was not just a narrative of absence but one of profound resilience.

From a young age, Jordan had been acutely aware of the void where a father's advice, discipline, and encouragement should have been. The weight of his reality could have easily steered him down a less ambitious path. However, Jordan's character—resolute and undeterred—spoke to an internal compass that guided him where a father's might have. His mother, a beacon of strength and determination, had instilled in him a work ethic that was as unyielding as it was inspiring.

How did he manage to rise above the statistics that often define young men in his position? I sought to unravel the fabric of his success, thread by thread. It was in the quiet moments of reflection, in the echoes of his mother's affirmations, that Jordan found the fortitude to press forward. Teachers and mentors recognized his potential, stepping in to fill the gaps left by an absent father. Their wisdom and guidance became the scaffolding upon which Jordan built his academic achievements.

Could it be that the very absence of a father had compelled Jordan to forge his own path with greater conviction? The unexpected twists of his journey painted a picture of an individual who refused to be defined by circumstance. It was a narrative that challenged preconceived notions, demanding that we look beyond the surface to the strength that lies beneath.

Jordan's story, while uniquely his own, touched upon a universal truth: the human spirit's capacity for overcoming adversity. His experience beckoned readers to look within, to recognize the resilience that resides in each of us. It was a reminder that even in the absence of traditional support systems, there is potential for greatness.

What wisdom could we glean from Jordan's narrative? The insight was clear: Success is not predetermined by the presence of a father but rather by the will to triumph despite his absence. It was a profound realization that promised to illuminate the pages of this book with stories of triumph and transformation.

Each anecdote within these pages serves as a gateway to understanding the complexities of black male student success. Readers will embark on a journey through the lives of young men like Jordan, whose shattered reflections have been pieced back together through sheer determination and the support of their communities.

As I, Samuel Essah-Hienwo, delve deeper into these narratives, I invite you to ponder the impact of resilience on academic success. How do the challenges faced by these young men shape their perspectives on education and their identities? What role do alternative support systems play in their stories? And, ultimately, how can we, as a society, foster environments that nurture and celebrate the success of all students?

The answers to these questions are woven into the very fabric of this book, offering a rich tapestry of hope, perseverance, and the indomitable human spirit. Through vivid imagery, engaging questions, and a rhythmic cadence, 'Narratives of Resilience' promises to be a compelling addition to the discourse on student success and social change.

Join me on this enlightening expedition as we unravel the hidden journey of academic achievement and the extraordinary young men who redefine what it means to succeed.

CHAPTER 2
The Color of Success

Redefining Achievement

What does success look like? This question, seemingly simple, echoes through the halls of academia, reverberates off the walls of corporate offices, and whispers in the quiet spaces where dreams are born and sometimes where they also perish. Yet, when we consider the unique journey of black male students, this question takes on new hues, shades that are often obscured by the blinding light of traditional metrics.

Success—it has been measured in grades, graduation rates, and the accolades that follow. But for many black males, these benchmarks can misrepresent the true essence of their achievements and, more importantly, their potential. How, then, do we carve out a space within the educational fabric that not only recognizes their journey but also honors their victories, both big and small?

The road to success for black male students is paved with myriad challenges and systemic barriers that strip away the very milestones used to gauge progress. This is the crux of our discussion, the central issue that we must confront with open minds and hearts. The prevailing narrative suggests that these students are failing by conventional standards, but what if the standards themselves are flawed?

Typically, we laud the valedictorian, the student with a full scholarship, or the one who lands a lucrative job straight out of college. We celebrate these achievements because they are visible quantifiable. But what about resilience, the overcoming of adversity, or the silent battles fought and won that never make it to a resume?

Here is where we diverge from the well-trodden path. The real solution does not lie in the abandonment of all traditional measures but rather in the expansion of our understanding of achievement. It's about creating a model that is inclusive, one that recognizes the unique strengths and experiences of black male students.

Imagine a framework that values the intangible—leadership within the community, the mentoring of younger siblings, or the balancing of multiple jobs to support a family—all while pursuing an education. These are monumental feats that often go unrecognized. Yet, they demonstrate a level of commitment and determination that is rarely captured by a GPA or a diploma.

To the educators, policymakers, and stakeholders reading this: consider how this shift in perspective could transform the lives of students you interact with every day. How might it alter the trajectory of a young man who feels unseen and undervalued by a system that does not reflect his reality?

The emotional weight of this conversation cannot be overstated. Behind every statistic, there is a story—a young man who carries the aspirations of his family who navigates a world that is not always designed for his success. By reimagining achievement, we honor their stories, and we invest in their future.

As we delve deeper, let's not shy away from the uncomfortable truths. The journey for black male students often involves navigating through a labyrinth of prejudice and low expectations. It requires a tenacity that is as commendable as any academic or professional accolade.

Herein lies an invitation to you, the reader. It is a call to engage not just with your intellect but with your empathy. To envision a world where the reflection of success is not shattered by biases and systemic inequities but is instead a true representation of one's perseverance and fortitude.

Now, consider the black male student who has mastered the delicate art of code-switching, who has learned to inhabit different worlds and still retain his sense of self. Is this not a remarkable achievement? It is these everyday victories, often unseen, that we must acknowledge and celebrate.

In this redefined view of achievement, the onus is on us to create environments where these students can thrive, where their cultural capital is acknowledged and where their diverse talents are nurtured. It is a call to action, a plea to look beyond the surface and see the potential that lies within.

To the young black men carving out their paths in this world: your success is not solely defined by the letters on your transcript or the salary in your offer letter. It is etched in the resilience of your spirit, the depth of your character, and the impact you make on those around you.

And so, we circle back to the question: What does success look like? It is as multifaceted as the individuals who chase it, as rich and complex as the myriad experiences that shape their journey. It is high time we shatter the limited reflections and pave the way for a more inclusive, more equitable vision of what it means to truly achieve.

RACIAL BIAS IN ACADEMIA

In the heart of a bustling university, where the collision of cultures and ideas should foster a vibrant tapestry of learning, a subtle chill often lingers—one that whispers of disparity, of a battleground where not all warriors are equally armed. Here, within these hallowed halls, lies our setting—a place of enlightenment that paradoxically casts long shadows of bias, particularly upon black male students.

Among the scholars and dreamers who roam this campus, we find Jamal, an astute and ambitious young man with a gaze set firmly on the horizon of success. His story, emblematic of many, unfolds as he navigates the academic rigors before him, yet it is the unspoken curriculum he must also master—the curriculum of survival against institutional prejudice—that defines much of his journey.

The challenge is as pervasive as it is clandestine; racial bias in academia does not always shout its presence. It sidles up beside you, cloaked in microaggressions, in low expectations, in the paucity of role models reflecting your image. Jamal, like many before him, stands at this confluence of aspiration and frustration where the color of his skin marks a divergent path replete with obstacles unseen to others.

The approach to confronting this insidious foe is multifaceted. Jamal, along with a coalition of peers and empathetic faculty, devised a series of initiatives aimed at dismantling the barriers erected by bias. They organized forums for open dialogue, mentorship programs pairing students with professionals who mirror their potential, and workshops on cultural competency for staff and faculty alike.

The results, though not immediate, began to ripple through the campus. Attendance at cultural events surged, fostering a heightened sense of community. The mentorship program saw success as students like Jamal reported feeling more supported and less isolated. Faculty members who participated in the workshops became more mindful of their biases, slowly altering the climate of their classrooms.

However, the true measure of impact resided in the nuanced shifts—Jamal, once reticent in the face of authority, now engaged confidently with his professors. His voice, once a mere echo in the lecture halls, emerged as a clarion call for equity, inspiring others to do the same.

Reflecting upon these strides, it becomes evident that the triumphs are as significant as they are subtle. The strategies implemented may not have completely eradicated the specter of racial bias, but they illuminated the path for continued progress.

Visual aids, though not present in this text, would include graphs of increased participation in cultural events and testimonials from students and faculty alike, further elucidating the narrative of change.

This case study, while specific to Jamal and his institution, is a microcosm of the broader narrative of black male student success. It serves as a beacon, revealing that the journey to equity in academia is not a sprint but a marathon—one that requires sustained commitment and the collective will to amend long-standing injustices.

Do we not owe it to the next generation of scholars to build upon this groundwork? To ensure that the reflections they see in the annals of academia are not fractured by the enduring legacy of racial bias but are instead whole and affirming?

As the author, Samuel Essah-Hienwo, my work is driven by the conviction that every student's success should be nurtured and celebrated. My scholarship and the initiatives I advocate for are a testament to this belief. My aim is not just to highlight the challenges but to forge pathways to overcome them—pathways that empower students like Jamal to mirror the success they so rightfully deserve.

So, as we turn the page, let us ponder this: How might the lessons gleaned here inform our approach to policy and practice within our own institutions? How will we rise to the call to action that echoes beyond the confines of this case study, resonating in every corner where learning takes place?

For it is within our power to sculpt an academic landscape where every student's potential is recognized and fostered, where success is not a privilege granted to a few but a right afforded to all. Can we dare to envision such a future? A future where our actions today forge a legacy of inclusion and equity for the scholars of tomorrow.

INSTITUTIONAL OBSTACLES

In the sprawling corridors of academia, where the pursuit of knowledge should be unencumbered by the shackles of prejudice, a silent storm brews. This tempest, though invisible to the fortunate many, relentlessly hammers at the spirits of black male students, such as Jamal, who strive to carve out their success against a backdrop painted with systemic barriers. It is these institutional obstacles that lay the foundation of our discourse—a foundation fraught with cracks that threaten to swallow the dreams of the unwary.

The primary challenge at hand is not one of individual malice but rather a more insidious and pervasive issue—the very architecture of educational systems that, through legacy and design, perpetuate disparities. Policies and practices woven into the fabric of educational institutions often operate under the guise of tradition and standardization, yet they inadvertently reinforce racial inequities. How, then, can one thrive when the labyrinth they must navigate is riddled with traps set by history itself?

Should these systemic barriers remain unaddressed, the consequences are dire and manifold. We face the gradual erosion of the promise of education as a great equalizer. The potential of bright minds like Jamal's could be forever dimmed, leading to a perpetuation of the cycle of inequity, where opportunity and advancement are stratified along racial lines. Imagine, for a moment, an entire segment of society repeatedly hindered from contributing their fullest to the common good. Can we afford such a loss?

The solution, while complex, begins with a commitment to equity that is both unflinching and proactive. We must first acknowledge these institutional barriers, bringing them into the light where they can be examined and dismantled. Then, we must redesign our educational structures to be truly inclusive, ensuring that policies, curricula, and support systems reflect and accommodate the diverse tapestry of student experiences.

Implementing this solution requires a multi-tiered approach. It starts with policy reform, such as revising admission criteria that disproportionately disadvantage black male students, and extends to the reevaluation of disciplinary procedures that often subject them to harsher penalties. We must also diversify faculty and administration, creating a reflection of the world students will enter upon graduation.

The efficacy of such reforms is not merely speculative. Institutions that have embraced similar changes report a marked increase in the engagement and achievement of their black male students. They tell of graduation rates climbing and of a newfound vibrancy in the classroom dynamic, where diverse perspectives are not only present but also celebrated.

Yet, we must not be naive to believe that a singular approach holds all the answers. Alternative solutions, such as targeted mentorship programs and student-led initiatives, also hold tremendous promise. These programs foster a sense of belonging and provide role models who demonstrate the heights that can be achieved despite the odds.

As we delve deeper into the heart of this matter, our sentences flowing like the very thoughts they represent—sometimes sharp and concise, other times winding and weighty—we must ask ourselves: What are we willing to do to ensure that the potential of students like Jamal is not left unfulfilled? How many more must brave this gantlet before we accept that change is not only necessary but overdue?

For it is through the collective efforts of policymakers, educators, students, and communities that the tide will turn. The reforms we envision must be sown with the seeds of hope and watered with the sweat of our perseverance. Only then will we see the harvest of our labor—a generation of students whose reflections in the mirror of academia are not shattered but whole and resplendent.

The path to this future is neither short nor easy, but it is one we must tread. Let us, therefore, arm ourselves with the courage to confront these institutional obstacles, for in their dismantling, we pave the way to a brighter, more equitable future for all. Can we dare to take this step? Can we dare to make this vision a reality?

In the end, the legacy we leave behind will be measured not by the magnitude of the challenges we face but by the tenacity with which we fought to overcome them. Let our actions today be the beacon that guides the scholars of tomorrow toward a horizon unmarred by the shadows of the past.

CULTURAL CAPITAL AND ITS ROLE

The essence of cultural capital lies in its invisibility; it is an unseen currency that permeates the academic halls, often determining the pace at which one navigates the educational landscape. Its role in shaping the trajectory of black male students cannot be overstated, for it is both a vessel for success and a potential source of inequity. To fully grasp this concept and its implications, one must first acquaint oneself with the language that brings it to life.

Embarking on this intellectual journey, it becomes imperative to elucidate the terms that form the crux of our discussion. Cultural Capital, Habitus, Field, Social Capital, and Symbolic Violence are not merely academic jargon but keys that unlock deeper understanding. The significance of these terms extends beyond their definitions; they are the threads that weave the fabric of our social world.

Cultural Capital can be likened to a toolkit of sorts, brimming with knowledge, skills, behaviors, and credentials society values. It is a form of wealth that one can accumulate and invest in the pursuit of social mobility. For black male students, it can be the difference between being perceived as a competent member of the academic community or an outsider struggling to conform to unspoken norms.

Habitus refers to the deeply ingrained habits, skills, and dispositions one develops through life experiences. It shapes how individuals perceive the world and respond to it. This concept is crucial for black male students, as their habitus is often at odds with the dominant cultural narratives found within academic institutions.

The Field is the social arena where the game of life is played. Each field has its own rules and demands specific forms of capital for successful participation. The academic field, with its unique set of standards and expectations, can be a battleground for those lacking the requisite cultural capital.

Social Capital, on the other hand, is the networks of relationships and connections that can provide support and access to resources. For students, it could encompass mentor relationships, peer groups, and familial support that contribute to their academic success.

Symbolic Violence is the imposition of a culturally arbitrary social hierarchy that is perceived as legitimate. It is symbolic because it is embedded in everyday practices and becomes naturalized. Black male students may experience symbolic violence when their cultural capital is devalued in the academic field.

Connecting these concepts to familiar scenarios enhances their relatability. Consider the game of chess as a metaphor for the academic field. Each piece has a role governed by rules that dictate its potential and limitations. Cultural capital is akin to understanding these rules and strategies, giving one the ability to make informed and advantageous moves. Habitus is the player's style, developed over many games, which can either align with or deviate from the standard strategies expected in tournament play.

In the game, social capital would be the network of fellow players and mentors who offer guidance, while symbolic violence is the unspoken hierarchy that can discourage newcomers from certain backgrounds from participating or feeling like they belong.

As these threads intertwine, they form a tapestry of understanding that reveals the hidden barriers and opportunities within academic environments. Black male students, armed with this knowledge, can better navigate the complexities of their educational journey. The realization dawns that possessing and augmenting cultural capital is akin to mastering a language that can unlock doors previously closed.

But what happens when the cultural capital these students bring to the academic field is undervalued or unrecognized? They find themselves at a crossroads, where adapting to the dominant culture might grant them success but at the cost of their own cultural identity. It is a delicate balance to strike and one that demands our undivided attention.

As we delve into the intricacies of these terms, we are not merely engaging in an academic exercise. We are shedding light on the lived realities of students whose potential is often obscured by a veil of systemic oversight. It is through this exploration that we come to appreciate the resilience and adaptability of those who continue to thrive despite the odds.

The canvas of academia is vast, and the brushstrokes that color it are as varied as the individuals that traverse its landscape. Each student brings a unique shade to the painting, a blend of cultural capital and personal experience that enriches the entire picture. The challenge lies in ensuring that every hue is valued and that every line contributes to the masterpiece.

Let us not forget that the discourse surrounding cultural capital is not an endpoint but a means to foster a more inclusive and equitable academic environment. It is about recognizing the diversity of experiences and the strength that such diversity brings to the educational tapestry.

In the absence of a traditional conclusion, let us instead carry forward the insights gleaned from this exploration. May they serve as guiding lights for the ongoing journey of understanding and empowering black male students in their quest for academic success. With each step, may we move closer to a world where every reflection in the hallowed halls of learning is valued and every journey acknowledged.

SUCCESS STORIES: BREAKING THE MOLD

The early morning sun crept through the gaps in the curtains, casting a golden glow over the small dormitory room where Malik sat, surrounded by a fortress of textbooks and scribbled notes. The clock ticked loudly, a constant reminder of the countdown to his final exams. Today was more than a test of knowledge; it was a culmination of a journey that defied every stereotype ever whispered in the hallways of his high school.

Malik was an enigma, a young man whose deep, thoughtful eyes seemed to hold centuries of wisdom. He was the grandson of a sharecropper, the son of a hardworking single mother, and the first in his family to step foot in a university. His path was not paved with the gold of privilege but with the grit and determination of someone who knew that education was the key to rewriting the narrative of his life.

As he turned the pages of his economics textbook, the whispers of doubt that had once echoed in his mind were now drowned out by the roar of his own potential. He remembered the teachers who saw a statistic rather than a student, the guidance counselor who suggested a trade school instead of college, and the myriad of low expectations set before him. But here he was, on the brink of proving them all wrong.

Malik's story was not an isolated triumph. It was a reflection of a broader truth that resonated with many of his peers—other black male students who carried within them the fire of ambition and the resilience to rise above the constraints of society's gaze. These were the young men who, despite walking through a world that often anticipated their failure, chose to carve out a legacy of success.

Among them was Jordan, a computer science prodigy whose code could dance across screens with the elegance of a classical composer. He had grown up in a neighborhood where the glow of streetlights often served as a beacon of safety and where dreams were commodities as scarce as a quiet night. Yet, Jordan's mind was a sanctuary of innovation, a place where algorithms and abstract ideas wove together in a tapestry of potential.

And there was Elijah, who could weave words together with the skill of an old soul poet. His spoken word performances left audiences captivated, hanging onto every syllable. He had faced his battles, both internal and external, with the might of his pen and the depth of his voice. His poetry was not just an art form—it was a lifeline, pulling him towards a future where his voice could echo in the chambers of change.

These stories, these young men, were the shattered reflections of a distorted image long cast upon black male students. Their achievements were not anomalies but the results of an unyielding will to excel against the odds. They were the embodiment of a truth that had been obscured by the shadows of prejudice and low expectations.

Why, then, does society continue to cling to the worn-out narrative of the 'underachieving black male'? Why are the success stories of Malik, Jordan, Elijah, and countless others not the first chapters in the textbooks of our cultural consciousness? The answer is as complex as it is uncomfortable—it is rooted in the historical soil of systemic barriers and societal misconceptions.

But the mold has been broken, the glass ceiling cracked, and the reflections of these young men shine brightly, illuminating the path for others to follow. Each step forward is a testament to their perseverance, each accomplishment a beacon of inspiration.

Can you imagine the strength it takes to stand tall when the world expects you to bow? Can you grasp the courage required to chase a dream that others deem unreachable? These young men do not just imagine it; they live it every day.

In this book, you will not just read about their achievements; you will witness the transformation of a narrative. You will see the power of self-belief and the impact of mentorship and community support. You will understand that the journey of these students is not just an academic quest but a profound movement toward social change.

Their stories are not merely tales of individual success; they are blueprints for a future where equity in education is not an aspiration but a reality. They remind us that when given the opportunity, support, and recognition they deserve, black male students can and do thrive.

As you turn each page, let the stories of these remarkable young men challenge your perceptions, inspire your spirit, and ignite a conversation about the true potential that lies within our educational system. Remember, the reflection that was once shattered has now been pieced together, offering a clearer, more accurate picture of black male student success.

This is not the end of the conversation; it is an invitation to continue the dialogue, to expand the narrative, and to celebrate the resilience and brilliance of these scholars. Their journey is a beacon that guides us toward a brighter, more inclusive future.

And now, dear reader, as you embark on this journey through the pages ahead, ask yourself: How can we foster an environment where more stories like these become the norm rather than the exception? How can we ensure that every young person has the opportunity to see their own potential reflected in the success of those who have come before them?

The mold has been broken. The reflections have been pieced together. The journey continues.

CHAPTER 3
The Policy Paradox

EDUCATIONAL POLICIES AND BLACK MALE STUDENTS

In the intricate tapestry of the American educational landscape, threads of policy weave patterns of stark contrast, particularly when one examines the experiences of black male students. These students navigate a labyrinth where each turn can be shaped profoundly by the policies and regulations set forth by educational institutions. In exploring this landscape, one's eye is immediately drawn to policies that are ostensibly colorblind yet, upon closer scrutiny, reveal disparate effects on students of color.

The purpose of this exploration is not merely to cast a spotlight on the disparities; it is to unravel the nuanced ways in which educational policies, both historical and contemporary, impact the educational journey and success of black male students. By understanding these intricate dynamics, educators, policymakers, and stakeholders can work toward crafting a more equitable educational system.

In establishing criteria for this analysis, we must consider policies related to school discipline, resource allocation, curricular content, standardized testing, and teacher expectations. These benchmarks provide a comprehensive view of the educational ecosystem and its multifaceted impact on black male students.

When we direct our gaze to the similarities between various educational policies, it becomes clear that many are underpinned by a rhetoric of equality and meritocracy. Policies such as standardized testing boast an objective measure of student ability and performance. Similarly, zero-tolerance discipline policies are often justified as a means to maintain order and safety within schools, applying rules uniformly across the student body.

Yet, when we shift focus to the contrasts, the inequities begin to emerge. Data consistently shows that black male students are disproportionately disciplined in schools, often for subjective infractions like defiance or disruption, which can be open to interpretation and bias. These disciplinary actions can lead to suspensions and expulsions, contributing to the school-to-prison pipeline that ensnares black male youth at disturbing rates.

Standardized tests, too, become a tool of stratification. The content of these tests often reflects cultural and socio-economic biases that do not account for the diverse backgrounds of test-takers. As a result, black male students may find themselves at a disadvantage, not because of a lack of ability but because of a test that fails to recognize their potential beyond a narrow set of parameters.

Visual aids, such as comparative graphs and charts, starkly delineate the disparities in disciplinary actions and test scores, painting a picture that words alone cannot fully capture. These visuals serve as a poignant reminder that behind every statistic is the story of a student whose potential is being curtailed by systemic inequities.

The analysis of these comparisons reveals a broader implication: educational policies often function as a double-edged sword. While designed to establish standards and order, they also reinforce existing inequalities, creating barriers for black male students that are often invisible to those who do not experience them firsthand.

The contemporary relevance of this analysis cannot be overstated. In an era of heightened awareness of social injustices, the call for educational reform grows louder. Stories from recent years highlight the struggles and triumphs of black male students as they contend with policies that do not always consider their best interests.

But how, one might ask, can this situation be rectified? How can the policies that govern our schools be reimagined to truly reflect the diversity and potential of all students?

Imagine a young man, eyes alight with the spark of curiosity, yet repeatedly told that his manner of speaking, his cultural references, his very identity do not fit the mold of academic success. This is the reality for many black male students, a reality that demands not just recognition but action.

In the past, adjectives and adverbs would have painted a picture of these students as "struggling" or "disadvantaged." But let us choose instead to see them as resilient, resourceful, and full of untapped potential. The language we use, just as the policies we critique, has power.

Consider the rhythm of a classroom where every student's voice is heard, where the cadence of learning is not dictated by a one-size-fits-all approach but by the unique needs and strengths of each learner. This is the goal for which we must strive.

Educators are on the front lines, armed with the knowledge that a single positive interaction, a moment of genuine connection, can ignite a student's passion for learning. They know that it is not enough to tell students they can succeed; they must show them through rich and relevant curricular content, through teaching practices that affirm their identities, and through policies that level the playing field.

As we continue to shatter the reflections of a flawed system, the journey of black male student success becomes less hidden, their pathways less fraught with unseen obstacles. The shattered pieces can then be reassembled into a new vision of education: one that reflects the brilliance and potential of every student, regardless of race.

THE EQUITY EQUATION

In the grand narrative of education reform, equity has become the drumbeat to which change marches forward. It is the cornerstone upon which we must build if we are to lift the veil on the hidden journey of black male student success. Yet, in the current educational climate, equity remains an elusive ideal, often confused with equality. Where equality aims to provide the same resources to all, equity demands that we acknowledge and address the individual needs and barriers faced by each student.

The issue at hand is not simply one of access but of nuanced understanding. Black male students, for example, often face a unique set of cultural and systemic challenges that can impede their academic progress. To gloss over these differences with a one-size-fits-all policy is to ignore the very real obstacles that these students navigate daily.

What happens if we fail to correct this course? The consequences are far-reaching and distressing. Academic disillusionment can set in early when students feel marginalized by a curriculum that does not reflect their experiences or by pedagogical methods that do not resonate with their learning styles. This disillusionment can lead to disengagement from the education system, perpetuating the cycle of underachievement and reinforcing the school-to-prison pipeline.

But what if we dared to dream differently? What if we crafted an equity equation that genuinely accounted for the varied needs of black male students? The solution begins with a commitment to culturally responsive education — an approach that uses students' own cultures as vehicles for learning. It requires educators to be fluent in the language and experiences of their students to serve not only as teachers but also as bridges to greater understanding and inclusion.

Implementing such a solution would necessitate a multi-faceted approach. First, we must invest in professional development for educators, equipping them with the tools and knowledge to create inclusive classroom environments. This investment would include training in implicit bias recognition and anti-racist pedagogies.

Second, we must re-evaluate our curriculum to ensure it is both inclusive and affirming. This means integrating literature, history, and examples that reflect the diversity of student experiences. When students see themselves in their studies, their connection to the material deepens, fostering a more engaging and effective learning environment.

Third, we must advocate for policy changes that prioritize equity. This could include more equitable funding models that allocate resources based on student needs rather than property taxes, which often disadvantage low-income, predominantly black communities.

Evidence of the efficacy of such approaches is not merely anecdotal. Studies have shown that when students feel represented and understood in their education, their engagement and performance improve. Schools that have implemented culturally responsive teaching practices report not only higher academic achievement among students of color but also a more positive school climate overall.

While these solutions form the core of our equity equation, they are by no means the only variables to consider. Alternative approaches, such as restorative justice programs that address student behavior through dialogue and community building rather than punitive measures, also show promise. Mentorship programs that connect black male students with role models in their fields of interest can inspire and guide them along their academic and career paths.

What emerges from these discussions is a vision of education that is as dynamic and varied as the students it serves. It is a vision that rejects the monochrome palette of uniformity and instead embraces the vibrant colors of diversity and individuality.

Take a moment to picture a classroom that truly embodies these principles. Can you see the walls adorned with the art and icons of various cultures? Can you hear the rich tapestry of voices, each contributing their unique perspective to the collective learning experience? This is the potential that awaits us when equity is not just a concept but a concrete reality.

As we move forward, let us remember that the path to equity is not a solitary journey but a collective endeavor. It requires the commitment of educators, policymakers, parents, and students alike. It requires us to not only speak of change but to enact it, to not just dream of a more equitable educational landscape but to construct it with our own hands.

For the black male student looking into the mirror of his educational experience, let his reflection be one of recognition, affirmation, and limitless possibility. Let us shatter the barriers that obscure his path and rebuild a system that propels him toward the success that is his by right. The equity equation, when solved, will yield more than academic achievement; it will unlock the door to a future where every student has the opportunity to thrive.

REFORMING FOR RETENTION

In a world where the potential of every student should be recognized and nurtured, we face a pressing challenge: increasing the retention rates of black male students. These young men often embark on an educational journey fraught with obstacles that many of their peers will never encounter. But imagine a future where these students not only persist but thrive, where their presence in graduation lines matches their representation at the starting gates of academia. This future is achievable, and the roadmap to reach it begins here.

The quest for enhanced retention is not merely an aspiration but a necessity. To embark on this quest, we must stock our arsenal with a deep understanding of the issues at hand, commitment from all stakeholders, and a willingness to institute bold, systemic changes. The necessary materials are not merely physical but ideological: empathy, courage, resilience, and an unwavering belief in the value of every student's success.

Let us first paint with broad strokes the overarching plan. The journey commences with a thorough assessment of the present educational landscape, identifying where we fall short in supporting black male students. Following this, we develop and implement targeted interventions, ranging from mentorship programs to curriculum reform. Each intervention is carefully monitored and adjusted, ensuring effectiveness and sustainability. The culmination of these efforts is a transformed educational environment that not only retains these students but also celebrates their achievements.

Now, let us delve into the details, each step a critical component of the larger picture. Our first endeavor is to create a supportive and inclusive campus culture. This means establishing spaces where black male students feel safe and valued, where their voices are heard and their experiences respected. Initiatives such as cultural competency training for staff and the integration of African American history and perspectives into the curriculum are vital.

Next, we address the financial barriers that disproportionately affect black male students. Scholarship programs tailored to their needs, along with financial literacy workshops, can alleviate the economic strain that often leads to premature departure from higher education.

Furthermore, academic support structures are crucial. We must ensure that tutoring, study groups, and writing centers are not only available but also welcoming to black male students. These resources should be staffed with individuals trained to understand and address the specific academic needs and learning styles of these students.

A sense of community and belonging can be fostered through mentorship programs that connect black male students with successful role models. These relationships can provide guidance, encouragement, and a clear vision of what is possible.

A word of advice: Do not underestimate the power of visibility and representation. Faculty and staff diversity are not just buzzwords; they are critical to creating an environment where black male students can see themselves in positions of knowledge and authority.

To verify the success of these initiatives, we will measure retention rates, academic performance, and student engagement. Surveys, focus groups, and interviews will provide qualitative insights into the student experience, ensuring that our strategies are truly effective.

In the course of this transformation, we may encounter resistance or setbacks. If initiatives falter, we must be willing to re-evaluate and adjust our strategies. Should students continue to struggle despite new policies, we must dig deeper, seeking feedback directly from those affected and being prepared to implement unconventional solutions.

Now, let us take a step back and consider the rhythm of our efforts. The process is not a sprint but a marathon, requiring sustained effort and dedication. It is a symphony of many instruments—students, educators, policymakers—each playing their part in harmony. The cadence of change will have its crescendos and decrescendos, but the melody must always move forward.

Imagine now a young man, his gaze steadfast upon the reflection of his potential. No longer is his image fractured by doubt or dimmed by systemic neglect. Instead, it is whole vibrant with the promise of success. This is the future we are working towards, where every black male student not only begins his educational journey but also triumphs in his pursuit of excellence.

The steps outlined here are not exhaustive, but they are foundational. As we implement them, let us keep in mind the profound words of Nelson Mandela: "Education is the most powerful weapon which you can use to change the world." By reforming for retention, we are not just changing individual lives; we are transforming the very fabric of society. Let us march forward with resolve, knowing that the work we do today will echo through generations to come.

CASE STUDIES IN POLICY IMPACT

Within the corridors of educational institutions, a silent transformation unfolds—a transformation guided by policies aimed at nurturing the latent talent of black male students. The journey to actualize their potential is complex, replete with challenges and triumphs that offer a microcosm of the broader societal shifts toward equity and inclusion.

In the heart of a bustling urban center, where the promise of education often clashes with the harsh realities of socioeconomic disparities, lies our first case study. Here, a public high school becomes the crucible for change, a place where the future of its students teeters on the precipice of hope and despair.

The school's leadership, a cadre of dedicated professionals, stands at the vanguard of this change. Among them Principal

Johnson, a seasoned educator with a deep understanding of the cultural nuances that shape his students' lives. His team, reflective of the community's diversity, includes policymakers, teachers, and support staff, all united by a common goal: to elevate the success of their black male students.

The challenge emerges from the shadows of historical neglect—achievement gaps, disproportionate disciplinary actions, and a curriculum that rarely mirrors the students' cultural heritage. These young men find themselves navigating an education system that seems oblivious to their unique circumstances and strengths.

A bold approach is crafted, punctuated by policy interventions tailored to dismantle barriers and construct bridges to success. The school district adopts a holistic strategy that includes the implementation of restorative justice practices to replace zero-tolerance policies, which have long funneled students into the school-to-prison pipeline.

The results begin to surface like the first rays of dawn after a long night. Disciplinary referrals plummet, and the students' engagement in their education soars. Graduation rates, once a source of despair, now climb steadily upward, painting a picture of progress that is both quantitative and qualitative in nature.

Yet, the reflection on this case study reveals a tapestry of complexities. Some argue that the policy changes are but a veneer over deeper systemic issues, a critique that invites further introspection and dialogue. As we analyze the data, we must ask ourselves whether our metrics truly capture the nuanced impact of these policies on the students' lived experiences.

Visual aids, such as graphs showing the decline in suspensions or the increase in college acceptance rates, offer a tangible representation of the strides made. They serve as beacons of what is possible when intention and action coalesce in the service of student success.

The narrative of this single high school extends beyond its walls, connecting to the larger discourse on the power of policy to shape educational outcomes. It stands as a testament to the fact that when the needs of black male students are met with targeted support, their potential is limitless.

As we turn the page on this particular story, a question lingers in the air, stirring the mind to ponder: What if these policy interventions were not the exception but the norm across the educational landscape? How many more reflections of success might we then witness?

The following chapters will explore additional case studies, each a piece of the mosaic that comprises the hidden journey of black male student success. Through these narratives, the goal is not just to inform but to inspire—to ignite a flame of advocacy that burns bright with the promise of change.

Imagine the corridors of schools nationwide echoing with the footsteps of students whose dreams are no longer deferred but realized. This image is not merely a hopeful vision but a blueprint for action. As we forge ahead, let us carry with us the lessons learned, the challenges overcome, and the conviction that each step taken is a step toward a future where every student's potential is recognized, honored, and fulfilled. The journey continues, and with each stride, we shatter the reflections of a fractured past, building instead a legacy of achievement and success that will endure for generations to come.

A Vision for the Future

Beyond the halls of that transformative high school, there lies an expansive vista—a horizon where the dreams of black male students are not just distant wishes but tangible realities. This is the promise I extend to you within these pages: an actionable blueprint that will not only inspire but also equip our nation to uplift these young men to unprecedented heights of success.

Imagine a future where policies are not just crafted but are also interwoven with the very fabric of our educational institutions, ensuring that every black male student is provided with the keys to unlock his full potential. It is a future where the tapestry of education is rich with the threads of their experiences, aspirations, and triumphs. This is not a mere ideal; it is a destination we can reach through the methodologies I will unveil—a composite of research, innovation, and unwavering dedication to social change.

Perhaps you are questioning how such a future is possible in the face of persistent inequalities and entrenched systems of oppression. It is a valid skepticism born of years of policies and promises that have fallen short. Yet, herein lies the strength of this endeavor: a rigorous, evidence-based approach that transcends mere rhetoric and is grounded in proven strategies for fostering resilience, academic excellence, and leadership among black male students.

Envision with me a journey through the annals of education, where each chapter of this book serves as a stepping stone towards a reimagined landscape. Picture classrooms that are not battlegrounds but sanctuaries of learning, where teachers are not gatekeepers but guides, and where curriculum is not a barrier but a bridge to cultural and academic enrichment.

In sealing this commitment with you, I am not merely offering a collection of success stories or abstract theories. Instead, I am presenting a living, breathing manifesto—one that breathes life into the aspirations of black male students with every policy enacted, every barrier dismantled, and every success story written. This book is a clarion call to action, a manual for those ready to be architects of a brighter future for these young men.

Let us delve deeper into the heart of this vision, where each policy is a chisel shaping the edifice of educational equity. From the implementation of mentoring programs that connect students with inspiring role models to the creation of culturally responsive teaching practices that affirm and celebrate black identity, the strategies I propose are both varied and vital.

Can we dare to dream of a world where schools are incubators of black male excellence? Indeed, we must, for this dream is the blueprint for the policies I advocate—a comprehensive approach that encompasses early childhood education, addresses the unique needs of black male learners, and fosters a college-going culture from the earliest years.

Through the pages to come, I will guide you step by step, revealing how each policy is not a solitary endeavor but part of an intricate network, all converging towards a singular goal: the flourishing of black male students. We will examine case studies, scrutinize data, and draw lessons from the frontlines of education reform.

And what of the doubts that linger, the hesitance born from past disappointments? They are the final barriers to be broken, the vestiges of a bygone era that we will leave behind as we march forward. With every chapter, your skepticism will be met with concrete evidence, your doubts transformed into a resounding belief in the power of change.

My credentials and years of research have not only provided me with insight but also with an unwavering conviction that this vision is attainable. As an accomplished scholar, I have peered into the heart of the issue, and with each published work, I have chipped away at the monolith of inequality.

Now, I invite you to join me in this endeavor. Together, let us cast the stones that will pave the path of progress, erecting milestones that bear witness to the innumerable successes that await. This is not just a journey we can take—it is one we must embark upon for the future of our black male students and the society that will be all the richer for their contributions.

A vision for the future is not a passive wish; it is a call to arms. It is time to pick up the mantle, to be the change-makers that will shape the destiny of generations to come. Through the collective efforts of policymakers, educators, parents, and communities, we can—and will—construct an educational landscape where black male success is not the exception but the rule.

As 'Samuel Essah-Hienwo,' I am not just sharing a perspective; I am imparting a legacy. A legacy that sees beyond the shattered reflections of a fractured system to a future where every black male student can look into the mirror of education and see his worth, his potential, and his success staring back at him. Join me as we embark on this hidden journey no longer. Our destination: a future unbound by the chains of inequity, where every reflection is whole, every dream is within reach, and every student's journey is a testament to our collective resolve to uplift and transform.

CHAPTER 4
The Mentorship Matrix

ROLE MODELS AND REPRESENTATION

In the tapestry of academic success, each thread weaves together to create a pattern of triumphs and challenges. For young black men, the hues of these threads are often cast in shadow, with their vibrant potential obscured by systemic barriers and societal misconceptions. Yet, there is a luminous strand that promises to redefine this narrative: the profound influence of accessible role models and mentors within educational environments.

At the heart of this revelation lies a simple but transformative proposition: that the presence of relatable role models can significantly bolster the academic and personal development of black male students. This assertion, far from being anecdotal, is anchored in a rich bed of empirical evidence.

Consider, for a moment, the journey of Marcus, a young man whose aspirations were ignited by the presence of an inspiring teacher. Mr. Johnson, a math instructor and a man of color, embodied the excellence and resilience that Marcus yearned to emulate. The connection forged through shared experiences and mutual understanding propelled Marcus from a state of disengagement to one of academic fervor. Mr. Johnson's mentorship was not merely a beacon of guidance; it was a mirror reflecting Marcus's own potential.

Delving deeper, we uncover studies that underscore this narrative. Research indicates that when black male students are taught by black male teachers, their likelihood of dropping out decreases significantly, and their interest in pursuing higher education escalates. The implications are profound: representation not only matters, it catalyzes change.

However, the path is not without its stumbling blocks. There are voices that question the scalability of such personalized mentorship and highlight the shortage of black male educators. They argue that the current educational system, with its deep-rooted inequities, cannot consistently provide these role models for every black male student.

In the face of these counterarguments, it is essential to consider the broader landscape of mentorship. The influence of role models extends beyond classroom walls. Community leaders, coaches, and even peers can fill these pivotal roles. Additionally, technology and online platforms are now bridging gaps, allowing for virtual mentorships that transcend geographic and systemic limitations.

Supplementing this, recent initiatives are actively working to increase the number of black educators, with scholarship programs and recruitment drives aimed at creating a more representative teaching force. These efforts, while not an immediate panacea, signal a commitment to structural change.

Stepping back into the light of our central thesis, we must consider the undeniable impact role models have on self-perception. A study from the National Association for the Advancement of Colored People (NAACP) illustrates how positive representation in academia can combat stereotypes, boost self-esteem, and broaden career aspirations among black male youth.

What, then, can we conclude from this mosaic of evidence and insights? It is clear that the presence of relatable role models and mentors serves as a vital catalyst for the success of black male students. Their influence not only nurtures academic achievement but also fosters a sense of belonging and identity, elements intrinsically linked to the perseverance and resilience required to navigate the educational journey.

In closing, let us pose a direct question: How might the landscape of academic achievement shift if every young black man could see himself reflected in the triumphs of his mentors? The potential repercussions are not just transformative; they are revolutionary.

Thus, we reaffirm our proposition, emboldened by the stories, studies, and statistics that weave through this discussion. The call for more relatable role models and mentors within academic settings is not merely a plea for representation; it is a strategic move towards dismantling barriers and constructing a future where the success of black male students is not the exception but the expectation. And in this future, their reflections are not shattered but whole, revealing the true scope of their capabilities and aspirations.

Building Effective Mentorship Programs

In a world where the educational odyssey of black male students is often fraught with systemic hurdles, the creation of effective mentorship programs stands as a beacon of transformative power. As we delve into the intricate process of nurturing these initiatives, we embark on a journey that promises to uplift, inspire, and guide these young scholars toward a horizon of untapped success.

The objective of this chapter is to elucidate a clear and actionable blueprint for establishing mentorship programs that resonate deeply with the needs and aspirations of black male students. By the chapter's end, you will possess a comprehensive understanding of how to cultivate a mentorship environment that not only supports but also celebrates the unique journey of these young men.

Before we commence this expedition, it is imperative to enumerate the prerequisites vital for the program's inception. These materials and conditions include a pool of dedicated mentors, a supportive institutional framework, funding for program activities, a participant recruitment strategy, and a robust evaluation system to monitor progress and outcomes.

Embarking on this voyage, consider the broad landscape you are about to navigate. The mentorship program will encompass several core phases: mentor recruitment and training, mentee identification and engagement, program structure and content development, ongoing support and resources provisioning, and finally, assessment and iterative refinement.

Diving deeper, let's break down each component. The recruitment of mentors necessitates a focused approach to identifying individuals who are not only successful in their respective fields but also exhibit a genuine passion for guiding the next generation. These mentors should reflect the diversity and experiences of the mentees, providing relatable role models that can deeply connect with the students.

Once the mentors are onboard, comprehensive training is essential. They must be equipped with the skills to build trust, foster open communication, and address the unique challenges faced by black male students. This training should also include cultural competency, conflict resolution, and strategies for academic and personal development.

The engagement of mentees is equally crucial. Outreach efforts must be intentional, tapping into schools, community organizations, and social media platforms to identify young men who would most benefit from the program. An inclusive environment that celebrates their heritage, culture, and individual stories is pivotal for their active participation.

The program's structure is the skeleton upon which all activities are built. It should include one-on-one mentoring, group workshops, and experiential learning opportunities that align with the mentees' interests and career aspirations. Additionally, creating a curriculum that incorporates life skills, financial literacy, and academic support will lay a multifaceted foundation for success.

Offering tips and warnings, it's important to highlight that flexibility and empathy are key. Be prepared to adapt the program in response to feedback and changing needs. Avoid rigid structures that stifle personal growth or overlook individual circumstances. A warning to heed: mentorship is a commitment, not a one-time event. Consistency and reliability in mentor-mentee interactions are the heartbeats of trust and progress.

To validate the success of the program, regular check-ins and evaluations are vital. These can take the form of surveys, interviews, and academic performance tracking. The feedback gathered will serve as a compass, guiding improvements and affirming the program's impact.

In the face of obstacles, such as mentor burnout or mentee disengagement, it's essential to have troubleshooting strategies ready. Offering continuous mentor support, recognizing and rewarding participation, and maintaining open lines of communication can resolve many issues that may arise.

Throughout this process, we have traversed the terrain of building effective mentorship programs for black male students. The vivid imagery of young men empowered by their mentors' wisdom and experience is not a distant dream but a tangible outcome of thoughtful and purposeful action.

Now, as we ponder the question, "What if every black male student had the opportunity to be uplifted by a mentor who mirrors his potential?" The answer lies in the pages you've just read: a comprehensive guide to cultivating such transformative relationships.

Remember, the strongest mentorship programs are those that evolve, adapting to the rhythms and cadences of the lives they touch. By integrating the insights provided here, you are not only contributing to the success of individual students but also sowing the seeds for a future where black male success is celebrated, replicated, and revered.

OVERCOMING MENTORSHIP CHALLENGES

In the landscape of mentorship, the terrain is often uneven, marked by unforeseen challenges that, if left unaddressed, can lead to the erosion of even the most well-intentioned programs. The path to nurturing black male student success is no less fraught with such impediments, where mentors and mentees alike must navigate a maze of complexities that can cloud the journey's end goal. Within this chapter, we cast a light on these obstacles and, more importantly, chart a course through them toward a clearer sky.

The principal challenge that often stands as a formidable barrier is the misalignment of expectations. Mentors, with their reservoirs of experience and knowledge, may enter the mentorship arena with visions of swift, transformative change. Mentees, on the other hand, might be seeking immediate answers to their myriad questions or even a paternal figure to fill deeper voids. When these expectations clash, the reflection of success shatters, leaving behind a mentorship bond strained and stretched to its limits.

What transpires if this misalignment is left unbridged? The consequences ripple outward. Mentees may drift away, disillusioned by the chasm between their expectations and reality. Mentors might withdraw, feeling ineffective or unappreciated. The program itself, once a burgeoning seedbed of potential, risks becoming a barren field where few relationships take root and even fewer flourish.

Is this the fate we accept, or do we dare to envision a different outcome? The solution lies in communication, a bridge built on the pillars of clarity and understanding. At the outset of the mentorship relationship, an open dialogue about expectations, goals, and the scope of the mentor's role should be initiated. This conversation is not a one-off event but a continuous exchange, a river of words that flows between mentor and mentee, carrying with it the sediment of trust and mutual respect.

To implement this strategy, we begin with the orientation sessions. Here, mentors and mentees engage in workshops designed to tease out their inner visions and align them with the program's framework. Mentors are trained to ask probing questions that reveal the mentees' aspirations and fears. In turn, mentees are encouraged to voice their hopes and what they seek from the mentorship experience.

The outcomes of these dialogues are carefully documented, forming a compass for the mentorship journey ahead. Regular check-ins are scheduled, not as perfunctory ticks on a calendar, but as vital touchpoints to reassess and realign expectations. As we weave these practices into the fabric of the mentorship program, we can anticipate a fortification of bonds, a harmonization of goals, and a reduction in the attrition of mentor-mentee pairs.

Yet, what of the mentors who face the specter of burnout, those who give tirelessly but find the well of their own motivation running dry? The solution emerges in the form of support networks. These are not mere gatherings but lifelines that connect mentors to peers, experienced advisors, and resources that rejuvenate their commitment. Mentor retreats, appreciation events, and continuous training sessions are not luxuries but necessities that maintain the vitality of the mentor's role.

Implementation of these support networks is detailed and deliberate. A calendar of events is meticulously crafted, ensuring regular opportunities for mentor rejuvenation. A mentor advisory board is established, composed of seasoned mentors who have weathered storms and can offer guidance to those navigating rough seas. Resources such as counseling services, stress management workshops, and time management tools are made readily available to prevent the flicker of mentor enthusiasm from dimming to darkness.

Evidence of the effectiveness of these measures can be found in the reflections of mentors who speak of renewed purpose, in the laughter that fills the room during mentor gatherings, and in the decreasing rates of mentor withdrawal. The predicted outcomes are mentors who feel valued and supported and who, in turn, impart a stronger, more resilient mentorship experience to their mentees.

While the solutions presented thus far are critical, they are not exhaustive. Alternative strategies may include peer mentoring programs, where mentees can also learn from and support one another, creating a community of mutual upliftment. Additionally, leveraging technology to facilitate virtual mentorship can bridge geographical divides and provide flexibility in scheduling.

The journey of black male student success is not a solitary trek but a communal voyage, where each challenge overcome is a collective victory. As we continue to break down the barriers and pave the way for meaningful mentorship relationships, we are not just mending shattered reflections but also piecing together a mosaic of triumphs that will stand as a testament to the resilience and potential of black male students.

And so, we ask ourselves: How will we choose to rise to the occasion when obstacles loom large? Will we falter, or will we fortify our resolve, ensuring that every young man who looks into the mirror of mentorship sees not a fragmented image but a whole and hopeful reflection of his future? The pages ahead hold the answer, but it is through our actions that the story will unfold.

MENTORSHIP SUCCESS STORIES

In the heart of a bustling urban neighborhood, amid the cacophony of everyday struggles and triumphs, there stood an unassuming community center that had become a beacon of hope. The walls of this center, adorned with vibrant murals depicting great leaders and visionaries, bore witness to the transformative power of mentorship.

Here, we meet Marcus, a youth with a gaze as determined as it is wary, and Mr. Johnson, an educator whose silver-flecked hair spoke of wisdom gained through years of experience. Marcus, like so many others before him, was navigating the treacherous waters of adolescence, his path obscured by the fog of societal expectations and personal doubt. Mr. Johnson, having dedicated his life to guiding young minds, saw in Marcus the embers of potential waiting to be stoked into a brilliant flame.

Their story unfolded on an ordinary Thursday afternoon when the community center buzzed with the footfalls of eager learners and the dedicated souls who sought to uplift them. Marcus, who had always maintained an air of self-sufficiency, found himself at a crossroads, the weight of his academic and personal challenges bearing down upon him. It was in this moment of vulnerability that Mr. Johnson approached, his offer of support as unexpected to Marcus as a lighthouse beam cutting through the night.

"Can you see beyond the horizon, Marcus? Tell me, what is it that you wish to find there?" Mr. Johnson's question pierced the young man's armor, prompting a torrent of unspoken dreams and fears to surface. To the outside observer, this might have seemed a simple conversation, but within it lay the seeds of transformation.

As their mentor-mentee relationship blossomed, the community center became their shared sanctuary. Through Mr. Johnson's guidance, Marcus learned to harness his intellect and creativity, his aspirations no longer tethered by the gravity of his circumstances. The walls that once confined him gave way to a universe of possibilities, mirroring the vastness of the night sky.

This tale, though unique in its characters and contours, echoes the experiences of countless other black male students who have found in their mentors the compass to navigate their journey. It speaks to the resilience that is forged in the crucible of genuine connection and unwavering belief in one's abilities.

As we delve deeper into these mentorship success stories, we uncover the universal truths that lie at their core. Trust. Empathy. The relentless pursuit of excellence against all odds. These are not merely abstract concepts but tangible forces that drive change that turn the tide in favor of those who dare to dream.

Within these pages, you will encounter wisdom distilled from lived experiences and insights that have been gleaned from the frontlines of mentorship. You will learn of the critical role that empathy plays in understanding the unique challenges faced by black male students of the transformative power of setting high expectations coupled with the necessary support to achieve them.

Through the tapestry of narratives that we weave, you will meet mentors who have become champions of change who recognize that their role extends beyond academic guidance to encompass life lessons that will stand their mentees in good stead long after they have left the classroom.

And what of the mentees? They emerge as architects of their destiny, empowered by the knowledge that they are not alone in their quest. With each victory, no matter how small, they shatter the misconceptions that may have once defined them, piecing together a reflection of success that is whole and unbroken.

As Samuel Essah-Hienwo, I invite you to journey with me through these pages to immerse yourself in the stories that are not just accounts of individual triumphs but a collective narrative of hope and perseverance. It is my deepest belief that through understanding and empathy, we can dismantle the barriers that obstruct the path to success for black male students.

Let us now turn the page and, in doing so, turn the tide towards a future where every young man can see his reflection not as shattered but as a mosaic of infinite possibility.

THE FUTURE OF MENTORSHIP

Imagine a world where every young black male has a mentor—a guide who not only walks beside him but also lights the way to a future resplendent with opportunities. This is not just a hopeful vision; it's a commitment to a reality that is within our grasp. By reading this book, you are stepping into a realm of possibility where the alchemy of mentorship transforms potential into extraordinary achievement.

In these chapters, the methodologies and strategies that will be unveiled are not merely theoretical constructs but are borne out of rigorous research and real-world application. These approaches have been carefully crafted to address the multifaceted needs of black male students, creating a scaffold that supports their ascent to heights previously thought unattainable.

Perhaps you're questioning, "Can mentorship truly make such a profound difference?" Let me reassure you: the evidence is compelling. Not only does mentorship provide academic and emotional support, but it also builds a bridge to the professional world, offering social capital that many of these young men might otherwise lack.

Close your eyes for a moment and picture a future where each black male student no longer walks alone. Instead, he has a mentor who not only believes in his potential but also invests in it, nurturing his dreams and aspirations. This future is not a distant dream; it is the journey we embark upon through this book.

Your engagement with this content is not passive; it is the first step in a commitment to changing lives. The stories and insights shared within these pages hold the power to alter trajectories and redefine what success looks like for an entire generation.

As Samuel Essah-Hienwo, my life's work has been dedicated to this mission. With a Ph.D. in Public Policy and Administration from Walden University and an MBA from Strayer University, I've delved deeply into the factors that foster student retention and success. The fruits of this labor are contained herein, ready to be plucked and savored by those ready to make a meaningful impact.

Now, let us turn our gaze to the horizon. What does the future of mentorship look like? It is a dynamic landscape, ever-evolving, shaped by the voices and experiences of those it serves. Mentorship programs are becoming more sophisticated, integrating technology and cultural competence to meet students where they are and guide them to where they need to be.

A mentor in this future is more than an advisor; they are a cultural liaison, an advocate, and a steadfast presence in the tumultuous sea of a young man's life. They do not simply impart knowledge; they are listeners, co-navigators, and, most importantly, believers in the boundless potential of their mentees.

In this book, we will explore case studies of successful mentorship models, dissect the qualities that make an effective mentor, and understand the nuanced needs of black male students. We will also delve into the psychology of mentorship, examining how a deep understanding of identity and self-concept plays a critical role in fostering resilience and ambition.

But this is not just about the mentees; it's about the mentors, too. What drives a person to become a mentor? How do they find fulfillment in this role? Through interviews and personal narratives, the motivations and rewards of mentorship are brought to light, offering a compelling look at the symbiotic relationship between mentor and mentee.

This journey is not just about success in academic or professional arenas; it's about personal growth, about the kind of introspection and self-discovery that shapes leaders. The future of mentorship is bright, and it promises to elevate not just individuals but entire communities.

By the time you turn the final page, you will not only have a deeper understanding of the transformative power of mentorship but also be equipped with the knowledge to become a beacon of hope yourself. Whether as a mentor, an educator, or an advocate, you have the power to contribute to a future where the reflections of our young men are not shattered but are a kaleidoscope of success, strength, and dignity.

Step forward into this shared journey, where the collective wisdom of generations paves the way for a future filled with promise and achievement. Together, let's unlock the doors to greatness for the next generation of black male leaders. The future is now, and it starts with us, with mentorship, with belief, and with action.

Welcome to the future of mentorship—a future where every reflection is whole, empowered, and brimming with the light of untapped potential.

CHAPTER 5
The Economic Enigma

Socioeconomic Status and Academic Achievement

In a world where the halls of academia echo with the footsteps of diverse lives, the intersecting pathways of socioeconomic status (SES) and academic achievement offer a convoluted map to understanding the educational journey of black male students. The terrain is uneven, marked by peaks of privilege and valleys of vulnerability, where the fiscal fabric weaves a pattern that often predetermines destiny.

What is it about SES that casts such a long shadow over the corridors of learning? At the heart of this inquiry lies the assertion that socioeconomic factors are significant determinants of educational opportunities and outcomes. The tapestry of an individual's financial stability, parental education level, and occupational prestige can either cushion a learner's journey or become a barrier that stifles academic progress.

The first thread of evidence supporting this claim is woven from statistical data. Research consistently reveals a correlation between higher SES and increased access to quality education— leading to better school readiness, higher test scores, and greater college enrollment rates. Students from wealthier backgrounds are often beneficiaries of enriched educational environments, from advanced placement courses to extracurricular programs, which foster both cognitive and social development.

Digging into this evidence, the disparities become more apparent. Schools in affluent areas tend to attract more qualified teachers, offer more diverse curricula, and provide state-of-the-art facilities. Contrastingly, schools in economically disadvantaged areas often struggle with limited resources, higher teacher turnover, and inadequate infrastructure, which can impede a student's academic journey. The chasm between the two realities speaks volumes, underscoring the impact of SES on educational attainment.

Yet, a closer examination reveals a mosaic of counter-evidence. There are narratives of resilience, where, despite economic constraints, students achieve academic success. These stories highlight the role of individual agency, supportive family structures, and community resources that act as catalysts for overcoming socioeconomic hurdles. They challenge the notion that SES is the sole arbiter of educational destiny.

In response, it's essential to clarify that while SES is not an insurmountable barrier, it does create systemic challenges that require additional support to navigate. The existence of success stories does not negate the broader patterns of disparity but rather illustrates the potential for triumph against the odds.

Further supporting this, evidence shows that interventions designed to level the educational playing field, such as scholarship programs, mentoring, and access to technology, can mitigate the effects of low SES. These initiatives can serve as bridges over the socioeconomic divides, proving that with targeted support, the barriers can be weakened if not entirely dismantled.

As we reach the close of this reflection, the reinforced assertion remains clear: socioeconomic status is a powerful influencer of educational opportunities and outcomes. The journey of black male students is not solely defined by SES, but it is undeniably shaped by it. The conversation must continue, unfolding the narratives that lie beneath the surface, understanding that every shattered reflection has the potential to be reassembled into a kaleidoscope of success.

The unyielding question then remains: How can society restructure the educational landscape to ensure that SES is not a determinant of a person's academic ceiling? As stewards of the future, it is our collective responsibility to seek answers to create environments where every student can gaze upon a reflection unmarred by socioeconomic fissures. Only then can we truly unravel the hidden journey of black male student success, piecing together the shards into a mirror that reflects the limitless sky of potential.

THE COST OF EDUCATION

The narrative of black male success within the educational sphere cannot be fully recounted without addressing the towering financial monolith casting its long, dark shadow over their academic aspirations. It is a structure erected from the bedrock of historical inequities, exacerbated by present-day policies and practices that disproportionately affect students of color, particularly black males. The cost of education, beyond mere dollars and cents, includes the price of dreams deferred and futures unduly burdened by financial strain.

The conundrum at hand is stark: the pursuit of higher education, a journey lauded for its promise of upward mobility and personal development, is fraught with financial barriers that disproportionately impact black male students. These barriers are not simply hurdles to be leaped over; they are pervasive, systemic issues that require exhaustive efforts to surmount. The financial obstacles embedded within the educational journey—from tuition fees to the costs of textbooks and living expenses—can deter even the most resilient and determined students.

Consider the aspiring scholar whose daybreaks are met with the balancing act of employment and study, whose nights are restless with the anxiety of looming debt. Imagine the young man whose potential is overshadowed by the weight of financial worry, whose choices are confined by the limited means at his disposal. This is the grim reality for many black male students. The impact is not merely individual but collective, as communities lose the immeasurable contributions of those who are forced to abandon their academic goals.

Take, for example, Michael—a second-year college student from a single-parent household in an underserved urban community. Despite his academic prowess and the encouragement of mentors, Michael's college experience is overshadowed by the specter of his mounting student loan debt. With each semester, the financial pressure intensifies, leading him to question whether his degree's promise of a brighter future is but a mirage in the desert of socioeconomic disparity.

The stakes are perilously high. The cost of education is not simply a barrier to individual achievement; it is a systemic impediment that perpetuates cycles of poverty and hinders the progress of entire communities. When black male students are forced to sideline their educational ambitions due to financial constraints, society is deprived of their potential contributions as leaders, innovators, and catalysts for change. The ripple effects are profound, touching every aspect of our social fabric.

Yet, within the pages of this book lies hope—a hope grounded in the conviction that these challenges are not insurmountable. Through the strategic deployment of scholarships, financial literacy programs, and policy reforms, we can begin to dismantle the financial barriers that encumber black male students. This book will explore and elucidate strategies to empower students to navigate the financial complexities of higher education, ensuring that the cost of education does not come at the expense of their success.

Embarking on a detailed exploration, we shall dissect the myriad of financial challenges, from the application process and the hidden costs of college life to the psychological toll of financial insecurity. We will delve into the narratives of those who have traversed these turbulent waters, gleaning insights from their journeys. What emerges is not only an understanding of the daunting financial landscape but also a blueprint for navigating it—a compass to guide students toward a future where their academic and professional aspirations are unencumbered by financial constraints.

As we forge ahead, let us ponder: What is the true cost of education, and how can we, as a society, invest in the futures of these students, ensuring that their potential is realized, not stifled? How can we reconstruct an educational system that equitably supports all students, regardless of their economic background? These are the questions that must be addressed as we seek to unravel the hidden journey of black male student success and transform the shattered reflections into a mosaic of triumph and achievement.

The road ahead is undeniably arduous, but it is a path that must be journeyed. In the chapters to come, we will examine the pillars of support that can uphold black male students, the institutional changes required to level the playing field, and the collective action needed to reshape the future of education. Together, we will uncover the means to repair the fragmented mirror, ensuring that every black male student can see their reflection whole and unblemished by the undue cost of education.

SCHOLARSHIPS AND SUPPORT SYSTEMS

In the heart of a bustling urban high school, where the echoes of ambition reverberate against the lockers, stands a young man named Elijah. His eyes, alight with the fire of untapped potential, scan the noticeboard peppered with flyers and announcements. Elijah, a senior with a transcript as impressive as the array of honors courses he's aced, harbors dreams that branch out like the mighty oaks in his community park. But beneath his scholarly achievements lies a sobering truth: the path to higher education is paved with financial tolls he's unsure his family can afford.

Elijah is not alone. He is one of many central figures in a familiar narrative, where the convergence of academic aptitude and economic constraint creates a poignant dichotomy. The core challenge these young men face is not a lack of talent or drive but the daunting cost of turning their collegiate aspirations into reality. For black male students like Elijah, scholarships and support systems are not just beneficial; they are essential lifelines.

The approach to addressing this challenge is multifaceted, encompassing individual initiative and institutional support. Elijah's journey to securing financial aid began with a diligent search for scholarships that cater specifically to black male students. He discovered a wealth of opportunities, from awards celebrating academic excellence to those honoring community service and leadership. These scholarships, often under-publicized and underutilized, represented more than monetary assistance; they were affirmations of Elijah's worth and acknowledgment of his potential.

As he filled out applications, Elijah also tapped into support programs designed to guide students like him through the labyrinth of financial aid. These programs, often spearheaded by educational institutions and community organizations, offer a range of services, including application assistance, essay writing workshops, and mentorship. They demystify the complex processes of scholarship hunting and financial planning, equipping students with the tools to advocate for themselves.

The results of Elijah's efforts were transformative. He secured several scholarships that covered a significant portion of his tuition and related academic expenses. The relief was palpable, as was the pride in his mother's eyes when she realized her son would graduate from college without the crushing burden of debt.

But the story doesn't end with Elijah's personal victory. The broader insights gleaned from his experience underscore the crucial role of targeted scholarships and support systems in leveling the educational playing field. Data supports the positive impact of such programs, with studies showing that scholarship recipients have higher retention and graduation rates. Furthermore, the psychological benefit of financial security cannot be overstated; it frees students from the incessant worry about money, allowing them to focus on their studies and personal development.

Reflecting on Elijah's case study prompts critical questions about the sustainability and accessibility of these programs. Are there enough scholarships to meet the demand? How do we ensure that information about such opportunities reaches those who need it most? And how can institutions better support students beyond the initial financial aid package?

Visual aids, such as infographics illustrating the distribution of scholarships and their impact on student success, could further illuminate the significance of these resources. By connecting the specifics of Elijah's journey back to the larger narrative, it becomes clear that his success is not an isolated event but part of a collective effort to foster equity in education.

As we consider the implications of Elijah's story, we are left to ponder a pressing question: How can we expand and enhance the network of support that turned one young man's dream into a tangible reality for many more?

The importance of scholarships and support systems in the educational odyssey of black male students cannot be overstated. Each award granted each program developed, serves as a beacon of hope, illuminating the path to success. It is our collective responsibility to ensure that these beacons burn ever brighter, guiding the way to a future where every student has the resources to reflect their true potential.

In the next chapter, we will delve deeper into the institutional changes that can further dismantle the barriers to black male student success. We'll explore the policies that shape the landscape of higher education and the advocacy efforts that aim to reform them. Our journey continues as we strive to piece together the shattered reflections into a vision of wholeness and possibility for every student who dares to dream.

ECONOMIC MOBILITY THROUGH EDUCATION

As the sun breaks over the horizon, casting its golden rays on the ivory towers of academia, we turn our gaze to a term that lies at the heart of many success stories: economic mobility. To understand its transformative power, particularly for black male students, we must first grasp its essence.

Economic mobility is the ability of an individual or family to improve their economic status, typically measured in income, over time. It's the proverbial ladder allowing one to climb from a lower economic stratum to a higher one, be it over a lifetime or from one generation to the next.

Delving deeper, we find that economic mobility is often categorized into two types: absolute and relative. Absolute economic mobility measures an individual's income in comparison to their parents at the same age, while relative economic mobility compares an individual's rank in the income distribution to that of their parents. Both aspects are critical in assessing the true progress of a demographic group.

Historically, the term 'economic mobility' has roots in the age-old pursuit of the 'American Dream' — the belief that anyone, regardless of their background, can climb the socioeconomic ladder based on merit and hard work. Yet, the black experience in America has often been at odds with this ideal due to systemic barriers and discriminatory practices that have limited opportunities for wealth accumulation and growth.

Within the broader framework of society, education is widely recognized as a crucial vehicle for achieving economic mobility. It's the engine propelling individuals toward better employment prospects, higher earnings, and the acquisition of skills and knowledge that can break cycles of poverty.

The application of this concept in real-world scenarios is evident when examining the lives of black male students who have harnessed the power of education to ascend economically. For instance, consider the story of Michael, a first-generation college student from a low-income background. Through scholarships, grants, and his unyielding determination, Michael obtained a degree in engineering. Now, he works at a top firm, earning a salary that has lifted his entire family to a higher economic bracket.

However, it is important to address common misconceptions or misinterpretations around economic mobility. Some may believe it is solely the result of individual effort, ignoring the systemic inequalities that can stifle ambition no matter how fervent. Others might think economic mobility is a given with any degree, not recognizing that the type of degree, the institution attended, and the network built during one's education can greatly influence outcomes.

The imagery of a ladder is fitting for economic mobility, but it is incomplete without acknowledging that some rungs are missing or out of reach for many. So, how can education serve as the reliable rungs that black male students need for their ascent?

Imagine a world where education systems are tailored to address the unique challenges faced by black male students. It's a world where culturally responsive pedagogy is the norm, financial literacy is part of the curriculum, and mentorship programs connect students with role models who have navigated similar paths. Here, education is not just a series of classes but a comprehensive experience that equips students for the economic realities ahead.

Can you see it? The classrooms buzzing with discussions that reflect students' lived experiences, the financial aid offices providing personalized counseling, the career centers designing initiatives that open doors to internships and job placements in lucrative fields. This is the kind of holistic educational environment that can transform potential into palpable economic gains.

Yet, questions linger like morning mist before the day's full clarity. How can such educational environments become commonplace? What systematic changes are required to dismantle the obstacles that impede the economic mobility of black male students?

In light of these contemplations, we must commit to a continuous examination of educational policies and practices, ensuring they are aligned with the goal of fostering economic mobility. For in the narrative of black male student success, each chapter of academic achievement is not only a personal triumph but a stepping stone toward a more equitable and prosperous society.

As we close this section, let us carry forth the conviction that education, when rightly aligned with the needs of those it serves, can indeed be the most powerful catalyst for economic mobility. Our collective task is to ensure that this is not a privilege afforded to a select few but a fundamental right accessible to all, paving the way for a future where every reflection of success is no longer shattered but whole and resplendent.

EMPOWERING FINANCIAL LITERACY

In the pursuit of economic empowerment for black male students, financial literacy emerges as a beacon of hope—a tool that illuminates the path to prosperity and autonomy. It is the cornerstone upon which a life of financial stability can be built. The goal is clear: to weave financial literacy into the fabric of education, ensuring that black male students are equipped with the knowledge to make informed financial decisions, navigate a complex economic landscape, and ultimately secure their financial future.

Before embarking on this transformative journey, it is imperative to identify the prerequisites. A comprehensive financial literacy curriculum must be developed, educators trained in delivering this material, and a supportive environment established where students can safely discuss and apply financial concepts.

Imagine a roadmap unfurling before you, each step marked with clarity and purpose. The broad overview of this roadmap begins with the integration of financial literacy into existing curriculums, progresses through the engagement of students with practical financial scenarios, and culminates in the ongoing evaluation and refinement of their financial acumen.

As we delve into the details, the first step is the creation of a tailored financial literacy program. This involves teaching the basics of budgeting, the importance of saving, the intricacies of investing, and the complexities of credit. Classes must be interactive, using real-life scenarios that resonate with the students' experiences and aspirations.

We cannot overstate the importance of practical application. Students should participate in simulations that involve budgeting for college, understanding loans and interest rates, and planning for long-term financial goals. These exercises serve as the proving ground for the theories they learn.

Here are some tips and warnings to consider: Ensure the material is culturally relevant and sensitive to the economic backgrounds of the students. Avoid one-size-fits-all solutions; instead, tailor guidance to individual circumstances. Remember, the objective is not to preach but to empower.

How do we validate that our efforts are bearing fruit? Success is measured by the students' ability to manage their personal finances effectively, their confidence in making financial decisions, and their pursuit of financial goals with diligence and understanding.

Yet, challenges may arise. Some students may struggle to grasp certain concepts. Others might feel overwhelmed by the breadth of information. When these issues occur, it is crucial to offer additional support, be it through one-on-one tutoring, peer-led study groups, or engaging financial workshops.

Now, let's bring this into sharper focus with vivid imagery. Picture a young man, eyes alight with understanding, as he realizes the power of compound interest. Envision a classroom abuzz with the energetic exchange of ideas as students debate the best strategies for investing. Feel the pride of a student presenting his first budget plan, crafted with the newfound knowledge of financial literacy.

Ask yourself: What if every black male student had access to this kind of education? How might their futures differ? How many dreams could take flight on the wings of financial competence?

Incorporate this quote from Nelson Mandela to underscore the message: "Education is the most powerful weapon which you can use to change the world." Here, financial literacy is not just part of education; it is the key to unlocking the door to a world of possibilities.

To reiterate, financial literacy is not just about money. It's about making strategic life choices, understanding the economic forces that affect those choices, and navigating the financial seas with skill and confidence. It's about shattering the reflections of a fractured past and stepping into a future where financial empowerment is a reality for every black male student.

In the narrative of 'Shattered Reflections,' financial literacy is not an elective; it is a fundamental right. It is the chapter where the potential is transformed into empowerment, where knowledge becomes the currency of success, and where the journey of black male student success is no longer hidden but heralded as a testament to resilience, intelligence, and the indomitable human spirit.

CHAPTER 6
The Cultural Compass

CULTURAL IDENTITY AND ACADEMIC IDENTITY

In the quest to understand the labyrinthine paths that lead to black male student success, one must consider the mirror in which they see themselves – a mirror that reflects not just a face but a complex tapestry of cultural heritage and learned academic self-concept. The intersection of these two facets of identity is a crucible in which success is forged or forfeited.

Grasping the essence of terms such as 'cultural identity' and 'academic identity' is like holding a compass in the wilderness. It guides us through the dense underbrush of misconceptions and stereotypes, allowing for a journey of discovery that is both personal and universal.

We embark on this exploration with a lexicon of critical terms: cultural identity, academic identity, self-concept, intersectionality, and resilience. These words are the signposts along the path, and understanding them is paramount to navigating the journey ahead.

Cultural identity is the sense of belonging to a group that shares common cultural codes and patterns. It's an intricate mosaic of language, traditions, beliefs, and values that shapes one's worldview and influences every aspect of life. This is the song of one's history, the rhythm of ancestors' experiences that beats in the heart of the present.

Academic identity, on the other hand, is often the reflection of one's self-concept within the realm of education. It is a narrative crafted from the grades on a report card, the nods of approval from educators, and the echoes of praise or admonishment in academic halls. It is shaped by the expectations and the perceptions of one's academic capabilities and potentialities.

Self-concept is the perception we have of ourselves, a mental picture that is constantly evolving with new experiences and information. It is the paint on the canvas of our psyche, colored by successes and shaded by failures.

Intersectionality, a term coined by Kimberlé Crenshaw, is the recognition that our identities overlap and intersect in ways that affect our experiences. It asserts that the cultural and academic identities of a black male student do not exist in isolation but are intertwined and compounded by each other and by society's perception of them.

Resilience is the ability to withstand and bounce back from adversity. It is the steel in the spine of those who face challenges head-on, the resolve that fuels the journey forward despite stumbling blocks.

How do these terms weave together in the real world? Imagine a young black boy in a classroom, his mind a fertile ground for ideas to bloom. His cultural identity informs his perspective, his voice, and the unique contributions he brings to the table. Yet, the academic identity that is often projected onto him by society may be restrictive, laden with biases that do not reflect his capabilities or aspirations.

His self-concept becomes a battleground where external expectations clash with internal aspirations. It is the answer to the question, "Who do I believe I am?" This is no mere academic exercise; it is a reflection of reality, of classrooms and playgrounds where young black men are writing their narratives amidst a cacophony of voices.

Intersectionality shows us that the journey is more complex that the student must navigate multiple identities – as a black person, a male, a student – each with its own set of challenges and stereotypes. It is the recognition that a one-size-fits-all approach is not merely ineffective; it is an erasure of the individual's multifaceted experience.

Resilience then becomes not just a desired trait but a necessary one. It is the armor worn by those whose identities are continuously questioned and challenged, the quiet strength that whispers, "Keep going," when the world seems to be saying, "You don't belong."

As we delve deeper into these terms and their interplay, we see a picture emerge – one of complexity, yes, but also of beauty and strength. It is the story of a cultural identity rich with history and wisdom, clashing and blending with an academic identity that is too often misunderstood or underestimated.

This narrative is not a simple one. There are no easy answers or quick fixes. But in the richness of its complexity, there lies potential for profound understanding and transformative success. The mirror of identity for black male students can be shattered by the pressures of society, or it can be a resilient reflection that integrates both their cultural heritage and their academic aspirations. The reflection can be distorted, or it can be clear, empowering them to see themselves as capable, intelligent, and worthy of success.

The journey is not over. The path ahead is still being carved by the footsteps of those who dare to tread it, armed with the knowledge of who they are and the unyielding belief in what they can achieve. In this landscape of shattered reflections, we find not just barriers to overcome but also the hidden journey of black male student success, waiting to be unraveled and understood.

Cultural Dissonance in the Classroom

In the heart of the academic sphere, where knowledge and culture collide, a silent storm brews. The classroom, a supposed sanctuary of learning and growth, can become a battleground for black male students navigating the treacherous waters of cultural dissonance. This discordance between the culture they carry within and the culture they encounter in educational institutions is not merely an academic quandary—it is the lived reality of many.

As the early morning sun casts its rays through the classroom windows, illuminating rows of desks filled with eager minds, one must pause and ponder: what happens when the education system fails to reflect the cultural backgrounds of these students? What are the implications when their voices are muffled by a curriculum that does not resonate with their lived experiences?

The problem is as clear as daylight; the cultural mismatch between black male students and the predominantly Eurocentric educational institutions they attend often results in these students feeling alienated, misunderstood, and undervalued. This is not just a gap; it is a chasm that can swallow aspirations and dull the bright spark of potential.

One might wonder, what are the consequences if this issue continues unaddressed? Picture a future where generations of black male students become disenchanted with education, where their talents go unrecognized, and their academic pursuits are abandoned. The loss is manifold—not only to the individuals themselves but to society as a whole, which is deprived of the rich diversity of thought and innovation that these students bring to the table.

But let us not dwell in the shadows of despair for too long. There is a beacon of hope—a solution that could bridge the cultural divide. Culturally responsive teaching is not just a method; it is a lifeline. It involves creating a classroom environment that acknowledges, respects and utilizes the cultural backgrounds of students as assets in their learning journey.

Implementing this strategy requires a shift in mindset and pedagogy. Educators must take the time to learn about the cultural backgrounds of their students, integrating this knowledge into their lesson plans and teaching methods. It's about creating a curriculum that mirrors the diversity of the student body, incorporating texts and materials that reflect their cultural narratives and experiences.

Evidence of the effectiveness of culturally responsive teaching is not mere speculation—it is supported by a growing body of research. Studies have shown that when students see themselves represented in the curriculum, their engagement, attendance, and academic performance improve significantly. They feel seen, heard, and valued, which in turn fosters a sense of belonging and encourages them to invest more deeply in their educational pursuits.

While culturally responsive teaching is a powerful tool, it is not the only one in the arsenal. Other solutions include mentoring programs that provide black male students with role models who share similar cultural backgrounds and life experiences and who can guide them through the educational landscape. Additionally, promoting family and community engagement in schools can create a support system that reinforces the value of education and bridges the gap between home and school cultures.

Each of these strategies holds promise, and their implementation could be the turning point in the lives of many black male students. It is a symphony of solutions, each playing its part to harmonize the discordant notes of cultural dissonance.

Imagine a classroom where the walls echo with the voices of students from all walks of life, where the curriculum is a tapestry woven from the diverse threads of their cultural heritage. This is not a utopian fantasy; it is an attainable reality. It is a place where the shattered reflections of black male students' identities are pieced back together, forming a mosaic that reflects their true selves—complex, vibrant, and brimming with potential.

The journey to unravel the hidden narrative of black male student success is fraught with challenges, but it is a path that must be tread with determination and hope. In the landscape of shattered reflections, we can find the shards of a mirror that once made them feel fragmented. With the right tools and the will to act, we can piece together a reflection that is whole, empowering them to see themselves not as the world sees them but as the architects of their own destiny, capable of carving out a space for themselves in the annals of academic success.

INCORPORATING CULTURAL RELEVANCE

In the panoramic quest to enhance the educational experience for black male students, the integration of cultural relevance stands at the forefront. It is a cornerstone that must be meticulously placed to uphold the archway of success and understanding. Herein lies a blueprint, a strategic guide to weaving cultural threads into the very fabric of educational pedagogy.

The quest begins with a fundamental goal: to create an academic environment that not only recognizes but celebrates the rich tapestry of black male students' cultural heritage. This environment will serve to reflect their identity, bolster their confidence, and promote academic excellence.

To embark on this transformative journey, one must first gather the necessary materials. Educators require a deep understanding of their students' cultural backgrounds, a diverse selection of culturally relevant teaching materials, and a willingness to embrace flexible and inclusive pedagogical approaches.

The broad overview of this process involves several key steps: conducting thorough research into the cultural backgrounds of students, curating a diverse curriculum, training teachers in culturally relevant pedagogy, and establishing a system of feedback and continuous improvement.

Delving deeper, each step unfolds with precision and care. Begin by engaging in meaningful dialogue with students, parents, and community members to glean insights into the cultural nuances that shape students' perspectives. Next, curate a curriculum rich with literature, historical accounts, and contemporary studies that mirror the students' cultural experiences. Training teachers becomes imperative here, as they must be equipped to deliver this content with sensitivity, relevance, and respect.

Practical advice is the compass that guides this journey. When selecting materials, aim for authenticity and avoid tokenism. Seek out authors and scholars from within the community who can provide genuine voices and narratives. Be cautious in addressing sensitive historical and cultural issues, approaching them with the gravity and respect they deserve.

The validation of this endeavor comes through the observable engagement and achievement of the students. Witness their eyes light up with recognition; their participation intensifies with relevance, and their academic performance soars with a newfound connection to the material.

Troubleshooting is an integral component, for the path is seldom without its obstacles. Resistance may come from various quarters — be it institutional inertia or a lack of resources. Overcome these challenges by building coalitions with like-minded educators and community members, leveraging evidence of success to advocate for systemic change.

Picture this: a classroom where the walls reverberate with the pulse of cultural pride, where each lesson plan is a thread interwoven into the students' identities. Can you see it? The reflection in the mirror gradually becomes less fragmented as cultural relevance acts as the glue binding together the broken pieces. The outcome is a reflection that truly resonates with the students, one that they can proudly claim as their own.

The journey to incorporate cultural relevance is not a sprint; it is a marathon that demands endurance, patience, and unwavering commitment. Yet, the rewards are immeasurable. As educators and advocates, we have the power to alter the educational landscape, to transform it into a place where the shattered reflections of black male students are made whole, where their success is not an anomaly but an expectation. Let us take up the mantle and pave the way for a future where every student can see themselves not just in the mirror of education but in the very annals of its success.

Celebrating Cultural Strengths

The sun hung low in the sky, casting a warm amber glow over the bustling courtyard of Eastwood High, where a group of students gathered, their laughter weaving through the air like a melody. Among them stood Michael, a senior with a bright smile and eyes that seemed to hold centuries of stories. He wasn't just a student; he was a living tapestry of cultural heritage, embodying resilience and intelligence that belied his years.

On this particular afternoon, Michael was the unwavering center of a circle of his peers, captivating them with an impromptu speech about the legacy of black scholars. His words didn't just echo in the courtyard; they seemed to reverberate through time, honoring the past and inspiring the future.

As the crowd listened, enrapt, Michael's voice rose and fell with the cadence of a seasoned orator, his narrative weaving through the triumphs and trials of figures who had paved the way for him. It was in this moment that the unexpected happened — a shift in the crowd, a sudden, collective nod of understanding. Michael was not merely telling a story; he was reflecting on their collective journey, embodying the cultural strengths that spurred them toward success.

His story was a mirror, reflecting a universal truth: the power of cultural identity as a catalyst for academic achievement. Michael's tale was not just one of individual success but a shard of a much larger mosaic, one that depicted the vibrant, enduring spirit of a community.

What wisdom could be gleaned from this? What insights did Michael's narrative promise to those who listened with open hearts? It was the understanding that each stride towards academic excellence was buoyed by the rich cultural currents that ran through their veins. It was the notion that every challenge surmounted was a testament to the enduring strength of their ancestors.

To truly celebrate the cultural strengths of black male students is to acknowledge the full spectrum of their experience — the vibrant traditions, the unshakeable family bonds, the oral histories passed down through generations, and the profound sense of community that fortifies them against adversity. These are not just abstract concepts; they are the very pillars upon which their academic success is built.

Imagine, for a moment, the impact of a classroom where these cultural strengths are not just recognized but are integral to the curriculum. Picture a history lesson that doesn't start with slavery but with the kingdoms of Africa, where students learn about Mansa Musa, the richest man who ever lived, whose empire was built on knowledge as much as gold.

Envision a literature class where the words of Langston Hughes, Maya Angelou, and James Baldwin are not just footnotes but focal points, their poetry and prose resonating with the student's own life experiences. Consider the power of a science lesson that celebrates the contributions of black scientists and inventors whose innovations have shaped the modern world.

This is not a dream. It is a vision within reach, a potential reality that demands not just acknowledgment but action. It requires educators to dig deep to not only ask what they can teach but how they can learn from their students. It calls for a curriculum that is as dynamic and diverse as the students it serves. It necessitates a shift from a deficit perspective to one that recognizes and harnesses the inherent strengths within black cultural heritage.

To the educators who hold the future of these young scholars in their hands, I say this: Let their cultural strengths be the lens through which you view them, not as students who need saving but as individuals brimming with potential, ready to be unleashed. Your role is not just to teach but to be a conduit for the wisdom that these students carry within them, wisdom that, once tapped, will spill over and enrich the educational experience for all.

For the students — the Michaels of every school — know that your cultural legacy is not just a wellspring of pride; it is a force of immeasurable power. Your history, your stories, your very identity are the keys to a kingdom of knowledge that awaits your claim. Embrace it, and let the world see the reflection of your potential, unshattered and whole.

As I, Samuel Essah-Hienwo, continue to delve into the depths of these reflections, I am reminded of the words of the great educator and philosopher, W.E.B. Du Bois, who said, "The function of the university is not simply to teach breadwinning, or to furnish teachers for the public schools, or to be a centre of polite society; it is, above all, to be the organ of that fine adjustment between real life and the growing knowledge of life, an adjustment which forms the secret of civilization."

Let us endeavor to be that organ of fine adjustment, celebrating the cultural strengths that not only enhance the academic success of black male students but enrich the tapestry of our collective humanity.

THE ROLE OF COMMUNITY IN EDUCATION

In the heart of an urban neighborhood, where the vibrancy of cultural murals stands in stark contrast to the fraying edges of neglect, lies Lincoln Community School. A place where the potential is abundant, and yet, the shadows of socioeconomic challenges loom large. This setting, emblematic of many across the nation, serves as the crucible for a story that transcends the walls of a school and touches the soul of a community.

Principal Jackson, a figure of unwavering determination and hope, stands at the helm of Lincoln with a team of educators who mirror the community's diversity. Among them is Mr. Richards, a math teacher whose innovative methods have begun to rewrite the narrative of black male achievement in his classroom.

The challenge was clear: Lincoln's black male students faced a torrent of low expectations and systemic obstacles that hindered their academic progress. Their potential was often overshadowed by stereotypes, and their achievements, when made, were seen as exceptions rather than the rule.

The approach was multifaceted. Principal Jackson and Mr. Richards spearheaded a community-driven model of education, one that sought to integrate local wisdom, cultural practices, and a profound respect for the students' backgrounds. They launched mentorship programs partnering with local black-owned businesses, invited parents and community leaders to participate in curriculum development, and created spaces for students to express their cultural identities freely.

The results were palpable. Test scores began to rise, but more importantly, the students' engagement and self-esteem soared. Attendance rates improved as the students found new relevance in their education, seeing it as a bridge to their future aspirations rather than a detached obligation.

Upon analysis and reflection, it became evident that the success of Lincoln's black male students was not solely due to changes within the school's walls. The transformation was rooted in something deeper: a collective affirmation that these young men were valued, capable, and deserving of every opportunity to succeed.

Visual aids were incorporated to reinforce this narrative—murals depicting black leaders and scholars adorned the hallways, and data visualizations of student progress were displayed, celebrating both individual and collective achievements.

This case study is but one thread in the larger fabric of the conversation around black male student success. It illustrates the profound impact that a community can have when it wraps its arms around its youth, offering not just support but a reflection of their worth back to them.

As you ponder the implications of Lincoln's story, consider this: How can we, as a society, replicate and expand upon such models of community and educational synergy? How do we ensure that the success of Lincoln becomes not an isolated tale of triumph but a standard for educational environments everywhere?

In my work and research, I have seen time and again that when a community invests in its youth, the dividends are immeasurable. It is not simply a matter of providing resources but of fostering an environment where black male students can see themselves not as marginalized figures but as central characters in the narrative of academic excellence.

We must ask ourselves tough questions. Are we prepared to dismantle the barriers that have long stood in the way of these students? Can we commit to being lifelong students ourselves, learning from the rich cultural legacies that our black male students bring to the classroom?

In one-line simplicity, the heart of the matter is this:
Community matters.

As we journey through the pages of this book, let us not lose sight of the profound simplicity in that statement. Let us remember that in the reflective surfaces of our endeavors, our students should see not shattered images but the wholeness of their being, the totality of their potential, and the unwavering support of their community.

So, as I, Samuel Essah-Hienwo, bring this chapter to a close, I leave you with a question that I hope will resonate in your mind and inspire action in your heart: What role will you play in ensuring that the cultural strengths and community support that drive student success are not just acknowledged but actively cultivated in our educational systems?

CHAPTER 7
The Psychological Pathways

MENTAL HEALTH AND ACADEMIC SUCCESS

In the labyrinth of factors contributing to the academic performance of black male students, mental health stands as a silent sentinel whose influence is both profound and pervasive. It is the invisible tapestry woven into the fabric of their daily lives, often overlooked yet crucial to their holistic success. Mental health, or the lack thereof, can be the fulcrum upon which the scales of academic achievement balance precariously.

What is the essence that binds mental health to academic success? How do these unseen threads pull tight the cords of concentration, motivation, and resilience necessary for scholastic achievement? To unravel this enigma, one must delve into the heart of the matter, examining the intricate dance between the psyche and the pursuit of knowledge.

The claim is clear: mental health is inextricably linked to the academic success of black male students. This assertion is not merely speculative but is grounded in a multitude of studies that cast a revealing light on this symbiotic relationship. The primary evidence emerges from research indicating that students with positive mental health are more likely to exhibit higher levels of engagement and to perform better academically.

Consider the findings from a comprehensive study conducted at a prominent university, where scholars investigated the academic trajectories of black male students. The data unearthed a startling correlation: those who reported lower instances of stress, anxiety, and depression not only attended classes more regularly but also participated more actively in their educational communities. Their grades, a tangible measure of their success, reflected this positive mental state.

Yet, to truly appreciate this evidence, one must dissect it, laying bare the components of mental well-being. It is not simply the absence of mental illness that propels these students forward; it is the presence of resilience, the ability to bounce back from adversity—a quality that is cultivated in a nourishing environment, free from the toxins of discrimination and stereotype threats.

The counter-evidence presents itself in the form of skeptics who argue that mental health is but one of many factors, perhaps overshadowed by socio-economic status or the quality of schooling. They point to examples of individuals who have succeeded despite battling mental health issues, suggesting that determination and talent can eclipse psychological distress.

In response, one must acknowledge the complexity of the issue while reaffirming the centrality of mental health. Yes, there are outliers, but they serve to prove the rule rather than to undermine it. Besides, success, in spite of poor mental health, often comes at a cost—a cost that could be mitigated by providing better mental health support.

There is additional supporting evidence if one peers into the realm of cognitive functioning. Mental health challenges can impair memory, decrease concentration, and slow cognitive processing—all of which are vital to learning and academic performance. When the mind is besieged by internal turmoil, the external world of academia becomes an uphill battle.

In drawing this exploration to a close, one cannot ignore the reinforced assertion: the mental health of black male students is a cornerstone of their academic success. It is a foundation upon which dreams are built and goals are achieved; it is the armor that shields them from the slings and arrows of educational adversity.

The journey of these students is not a solitary one; it is a shared voyage with mental health as their compass. To ensure that they do not navigate these waters alone, society must commit to supporting their mental well-being, for it is in the reflection of their minds that their true potential is seen, not shattered, but shining with unyielding promise.

ADDRESSING STIGMA AND ACCESS TO CARE

In the tapestry of black male students' lives, there is a thread that is often invisible yet significantly impacts their journey to success—mental health. The stigma attached to mental health issues is a pervasive and insidious force, causing many to suffer in silence. This reluctance to seek help, compounded by barriers to access care, can derail the educational and personal growth of these individuals. But what happens when the silence is broken when the barriers are dismantled? What transformations could unfold?

The context of this issue is rooted deeply in societal misconceptions and prejudices. Historically, mental health challenges in the black community have been met with skepticism and derision. This stigma is a formidable opponent, a shadow that casts doubt on the legitimacy of mental health struggles and often discourages individuals from seeking the assistance they need.

Black male students face a unique set of challenges in this arena. Cultural expectations of masculinity, coupled with racial stereotypes, can create a double bind, trapping them between the need for support and the fear of being perceived as weak or incapable. This perception is not just internalized; it is mirrored and magnified by society's gaze, further entrenching the stigma.

The consequences of unaddressed mental health issues are manifold. Academic performance can plummet as students grapple internally with issues that go unseen. Relationships may suffer, isolation can increase, and the potential for self-harm or substance abuse rises. The long-term implications extend beyond the classroom, potentially affecting career opportunities and life satisfaction.

The solution, therefore, must be multifaceted, tackling both the stigma and the barriers to accessing care. One promising method is the implementation of culturally sensitive mental health programs within educational institutions. These programs would not only offer support but also educate, empowering students to recognize and address mental health concerns.

How, then, can such programs be put into action? First, educational institutions must partner with mental health professionals who understand the cultural nuances of the black community. Together, they can create safe spaces where students feel comfortable discussing their mental health without fear of judgment or retribution.

These programs could also employ peer-to-peer support systems, training students to recognize signs of mental distress in themselves and others and to provide initial support and guidance toward professional resources. By normalizing these conversations among their peers, the stigma can begin to erode.

But how effective are these solutions? Evidence shows that when students have access to mental health resources that resonate with their cultural experiences, they are more likely to engage with those services and report improved mental well-being. Furthermore, schools that have implemented such programs have observed a positive shift in the overall campus culture regarding mental health.

While the proposed solutions hold promise, it is also crucial to consider alternatives. Some suggest that broader community outreach, including mentorship programs that extend beyond school boundaries, could provide additional layers of support. Others advocate for increased online resources, which can offer anonymity and ease of access.

In the quiet before dawn, a black male student sits, his mind racing with thoughts unspoken. The weight of expectation bears down on him, a silent plea for help escaping into the void. Can you imagine his relief when he discovers a place where his voice can be heard, where his struggles are acknowledged, and support is readily available?

Institutions have the power to break the cycle of stigma and limited access to care. By taking decisive action, they can foster an environment where black male students thrive academically and emotionally. The journey towards dismantling these barriers is not an easy one, but it is necessary. The reflection in the mirror need not be shattered; it can be whole, strong, and resilient, just like the students it represents.

HOLISTIC SUPPORT STRUCTURES

As we delve into the labyrinth of the human psyche, particularly that of black male students, we begin to understand the necessity of comprehensive support systems. These systems are designed to nurture not only the intellect but the spirit as well, creating a sanctuary where mental well-being is paramount. To achieve this harmonious state, where the mind is attended to with the same vigor as academic pursuits, a sequential roadmap of actions is laid out before us.

The objective here is clear: to forge a robust framework that supports the mental well-being of black male students, ensuring their success both within and beyond the educational realm. To bring this vision to life, an assemblage of resources must be laid at our feet, including culturally competent mental health professionals, peer-support networks, and institutions willing to embrace change.

Imagine, if you will, a broad canopy under which these students can find shelter—a series of steps that lead them from the shadow of stigma into the light of understanding and acceptance. At its core, this process involves the identification of needs, the creation of responsive programs, and the fostering of a community that champions mental health awareness.

As we embark on this journey, it's crucial to dissect each phase with meticulous care. Our first step is to cultivate an environment where mental health is openly discussed and valued. Schools and universities can ignite this transformation by hosting seminars and workshops that destigmatize mental health issues, particularly those faced by black male students. Here, the experiences and challenges unique to these students are brought to the forefront, creating a platform for empathy and action.

Next, we must harness the power of representation. By employing counselors and mental health advocates who mirror the demographic they serve, a bridge of trust is formed. These professionals can adeptly navigate the cultural nuances that may otherwise be overlooked, offering students a reflection of themselves and affirming that their experiences are seen and understood.

Peer-support networks emerge as a beacon of solidarity, illuminating the path for those who may otherwise wander in isolation. Training sessions for these peer mentors are crucial— they equip students with the tools to recognize signs of mental distress and provide a compassionate ear and guidance toward professional help.

In the tapestry of this intricate system, practical advice weaves its way through the fabric. Students are encouraged to engage in self-care practices, such as mindfulness and exercise, which serve as vital supplements to formal support structures. Meanwhile, institutions are urged to integrate mental health education into their curricula, embedding the importance of psychological well-being alongside academic achievement.

How do we measure the success of these endeavors? Validation comes in the form of increased engagement with mental health services, a noticeable decline in the stigma surrounding mental health discussions, and, most importantly, the personal testimonials of students who have found solace and strength through these support systems.

Yet, we must acknowledge that no system is infallible. Challenges may arise, such as resource limitations or resistance to cultural shifts within institutions. In these instances, a troubleshooting guide becomes an invaluable tool, offering solutions such as seeking community partnerships to expand services or employing innovative approaches like digital counseling platforms.

In the quiet corridors of the mind, where once turmoil reigned, there now exists a possibility for peace. A black male student, previously engulfed in the silence of his struggles, now steps forward into a space where his voice echoes with the stories of many. Here, he is understood, supported, and empowered.

An institution that commits to such comprehensive support systems is not merely an academic setting; it transforms into a crucible of growth, resilience, and success. The reflection that was once shattered now reveals a mosaic of experiences—each piece a testament to the strength that comes from holistic support.

RESILIENCE AND COPING MECHANISMS

Under the golden blaze of a setting sun, Malik trudged through the campus with a weight much heavier than the backpack that clung to his shoulders. The weight of expectation, of history, of a future not yet written, bore down upon him with relentless gravity. Each step was a testament to the resilience ingrained in his DNA, passed down through generations who had navigated far harsher realities.

Malik, a sophomore at a prestigious university, was the embodiment of hope for his family. His mother's eyes often glistened with unshed tears of pride, and his younger siblings watched him with a reverence reserved for heroes of old. Yet, beneath his calm exterior, the tumultuous sea of academic pressure and racial tension surged.

In classrooms where he was often the only black male, the gazes that met him were a blend of curiosity and indifference. His presence was an anomaly, his intellect a surprise. It was in these moments of unspoken challenge that Malik's story diverged from what one might expect.

He found solace in the quietness of the library amidst the scent of aged books and the soft symphony of fingers dancing on keyboards. Here, he would plunge into the academic texts but also into the writings of James Baldwin and Ta-Nehisi Coates, drawing strength from their words. They spoke of struggle, yes, but also of the power and beauty of blackness.

"Whose world is this?" Malik would often ponder, echoing the lyrics that hummed through his earphones. The campus was a world away from the neighborhood he called home, and yet here he was, carving out a place for himself with every essay, every project, every exam.

When the strain of invisibility threatened to shroud him, Malik turned to mentorship. Dr. James, a professor who had navigated similar paths, became a beacon. Their conversations, often laced with laughter, sometimes with frustration, were anchors in the choppy waters of academia. Dr. James shared tales of his own journey, the barriers he'd hurdled, and the resilience he'd fortified along the way.

This mentorship was a mirror in which Malik could see his own potential reflected back at him. The message was clear: "You belong here, as much as anyone. Your voice matters."

Malik's coping mechanisms were as varied as the challenges he faced. He sought refuge in the rhythm of his poetry, in the release of the basketball court, in the fellowship of his peers. These moments of reprieve were not escapes from reality but fuel for the journey.

He also embraced the power of vulnerability, joining a support group where black male students gathered to shed the armor society often forced them to wear. In this circle of trust, they shared their fears, their dreams, and their strategies for survival. This was a sacred space where laughter could heal and tears did not signify weakness.

Engaging in these groups, Malik discovered the transformative power of collective resilience. The group's mantra, "Lift as we climb," became a guiding principle, a reminder that their individual successes were pieces of a larger puzzle.

What does it mean to thrive in an environment that was not designed with you in mind? For Malik and his peers, it meant rewriting the narrative asserting their place in the academic world with a quiet but unyielding determination. It meant honoring the legacy of those who came before them by reaching back to uplift others.

The reader, following Malik's journey, is invited to consider these threads of resilience that weave through the tapestry of black male student success. It's a story of triumph, not just over external adversities but also over the internalized narratives that threaten to limit potential.

Malik's story is a single thread in a vast and intricate fabric. It speaks to the universal struggle for recognition, for understanding, and for success on one's own terms. It is a testament to the resilience that is not simply about enduring but about thriving, transforming, and transcending.

As you journey through these pages, you, the reader, will uncover the strategies that have enabled students like Malik to navigate through turbulent waters and emerge not just unscathed but victorious. Their reflections, once shattered by the misconceptions and prejudices of the world, now come together to form a clearer, stronger image of what it means to succeed against all odds.

And so, I invite you to delve deeper into these narratives, to uncover the wisdom that lies within and to carry it with you as a beacon of hope and a blueprint for change. For in understanding their journey, we come to understand the very essence of what it means to be resilient.

FOSTERING EMOTIONAL INTELLIGENCE

As dawn's early light filters through the curtains of a modest dorm room, Xavier, like Malik, begins his day not with the usual hum of an alarm clock but with the soft, mindful chimes from an app on his phone designed to cultivate mindfulness and emotional awareness. This ritual sets the tone for a day lived with intention and emotional clarity. It is within this framework of fostering emotional intelligence that our narrative unfolds, illuminating the path to nurturing a vital component of education for black male students like Xavier.

The pursuit here is clear: to equip young black men with the emotional intelligence necessary to navigate the complex social and academic landscapes they encounter. The aim is to empower them with self-awareness, self-regulation, motivation, empathy, and social skills that form the bedrock of emotional intelligence. With these tools, students like Xavier can face challenges with resilience, form meaningful relationships, and achieve remarkable success in their personal and academic lives.

To embark on this transformative journey, a few prerequisites are essential. First, an environment that supports emotional learning is crucial. This includes access to mentors, educators, and counselors who value and understand the importance of emotional development. Second, resources such as books, workshops, and programs that focus on emotional intelligence must be made available. Finally, a personal commitment from students to engage with these materials and apply what they learn is indispensable.

The roadmap to fostering emotional intelligence begins by creating awareness of emotions and then teaching the management and harnessing of these emotions for positive outcomes. It involves understanding and empathizing with others and developing strong relationship skills. The journey continues with learning how to apply these skills in real-world situations, from the classroom to the broader community setting.

First, students engage in activities that promote self-awareness. Workshops that involve journaling, reflective exercises, and mindfulness practices help students recognize their emotional states and triggers. This self-discovery is the foundation upon which other emotional skills are built.

Next, self-regulation strategies are introduced. Techniques such as deep breathing, meditation, and positive self-talk enable students to manage stress and regulate their emotional responses.

This step is crucial in a world that often responds to the expressions of black male emotions with negativity or fear.

Motivation is fostered by setting personal goals and identifying intrinsic values that drive behavior. This inner drive becomes the engine for academic perseverance and the pursuit of long-term aspirations.

Empathy development comes from engaging in active listening exercises, role-playing scenarios, and community service. These activities teach students to understand and share the feelings of others, a skill that enhances their social interactions and supports their roles as compassionate leaders.

Finally, students are encouraged to cultivate strong social skills. Group projects, peer mentoring, and extracurricular activities offer practical opportunities to practice effective communication, conflict resolution, and teamwork.

Navigating the emotional landscape requires patience and practice. Encourage students to be gentle with themselves as they learn and grow. However, they must also be aware of the societal stigmas that wrongly associate vulnerability with weakness, especially for black men. It is vital to challenge these misconceptions and create new narratives around strength and emotion.

Students can measure their growth in emotional intelligence through self-assessments, feedback from peers and mentors, and personal reflection. Improvement might not always be linear, but the gradual ability to handle emotional challenges with grace is a clear sign of progress.

When students encounter obstacles, such as difficulty in managing emotions or setbacks in their relationships, it is important to seek support. Regular check-ins with mentors, participation in support groups, and even professional counseling can provide guidance and reassurance.

In the quiet of the evening, Xavier reflects on his day. The moments of triumph over frustration, the shared laughter with a friend, and the difficult conversation that led to mutual understanding—all are evidence of his growing emotional intelligence. And so, the journey continues, not just for Xavier but for all who walk this path, a journey of self-discovery and empowerment that reverberates far beyond the walls of academia into the very essence of their lives.

CHAPTER 8
The Call to Action

Mobilizing for Change

This book will serve as a beacon, guiding you through the stormy waters of societal indifference and systemic barriers toward the shores of empowerment for black male students. You are about to embark on a journey that promises more than just insights—it offers a blueprint for action, a catalyst for change, and a testament to the resilience of the human spirit. Here, within these pages, lies not just a book but a movement, one that will stir the soul and awaken the collective conscience.

Dive into a treasure trove of methodologies meticulously crafted from years of research and hands-on experience. Drawing on public policy frameworks, educational theories, and the power of grassroots activism, we will explore how to build robust support systems, foster empowering educational environments, and dismantle the structural roadblocks that impede black male success. The strategies you'll discover are both innovative and grounded, born from the real-world challenges and triumphs of those who've walked this path.

Perhaps you're skeptical, wondering how yet another book can make a dent in an issue so deeply entrenched in our institutions and societal fabric. You may ask, "Can words truly inspire action and lead to tangible results?" To you, I say, witness the power of informed, passionate advocacy, underscored by evidence and driven by a profound belief in human potential. This is not just academic musings; it's a call to arms backed by a track record of sparking dialogue and inciting progress.

Envision the transformation not as a distant dream but as an unfolding reality. Picture a world where black male students are not just surviving but thriving, their potential unleashed for the

123

benefit of all. Imagine classrooms that are incubators for excellence, communities united in support, and policies that pave the way for success. This is the world we're building—one page, one mind, one heart at a time.

Your commitment to reading this book is more than an investment in knowledge; it's an endorsement of hope and a step toward a more equitable future. By turning each page, you reinforce the value of every black male student's journey and your own role in shaping a world where their success is the rule, not the exception.

With vivid imagery, let us paint the canvas of possibility. Picture a young man standing at the crossroads of opportunity and obstacle, his gaze fixed on a horizon that seems perpetually out of reach. Now, see him surrounded by a legion of allies, educators, policymakers, and peers, all extending a hand to lift him toward his destiny. This is the future we strive for, and it's within our grasp.

Does the thought of such transformation ignite a fire within you? It should, for the embers of change are fanned by our collective breath, our words, our actions. Each chapter you explore will stoke this fire, fueling a passionate quest for justice and opportunity.

Now, consider the power of a single question posed directly to you, the reader: What role will you play in this pivotal moment of change? Your answer could shape the lives of countless individuals, molding the future in ways you've yet to imagine.

In our pursuit of potency over platitude, we choose nouns and verbs that resonate with strength and purpose. Our language is our sword, cutting through the noise and reaching the heart of the matter with clarity and conviction.

Sometimes, it's a one-line paragraph that lands with the weight of a thousand words:

CHANGE BEGINS WITH YOU.

Simple language ensures our message is not lost in translation, inviting a broad audience to partake in this crucial conversation. The cadence of our sentences dances to the rhythm of urgency and inspiration, a symphony of hope composed with every syllable.

Quotations from leaders and dialogues from within the trenches of education add authenticity and depth, echoing the collective voice of a community yearning for change. "Education is the passport to the future," Malcolm X once declared, and we hold that passport in our hands, ready to stamp it with the seal of action.

We choose to show, not tell, offering anecdotes that breathe life into statistics, stories that illuminate pathways of success, and faces that reflect the dreams and determination of a generation. These are not mere reflections; they are windows into souls, into lives that matter, into a future that demands our unwavering commitment.

Mobilizing for Change is more than just a chapter in a book; it's a chapter in history. Let's write it together, with a pen dipped in the ink of passion and a narrative that bends inexorably toward justice.

This is our time. This is our cause. This is our mission.

Are you ready to join the movement?

STRATEGIES FOR EDUCATORS

Embarking on the quest to cultivate an inclusive and supportive learning environment demands more than good intentions; it requires a concrete plan of action. Educators who traverse this path play a pivotal role in shaping the experience and outcomes of black male students. Here lies a sequential roadmap, a guiding light for those committed to nurturing the seeds of success within these young minds.

The objective is clear: To equip educators with the tools to foster an environment where every black male student can flourish academically and personally. To achieve this, one must first understand the prerequisites. A deep knowledge of cultural competencies, an awareness of unconscious biases, and the readiness to implement differentiated instruction are foundational. These are not mere boxes to tick; they are the bedrock upon which we build.

Picture a mosaic of strategies, each piece essential, together forming a masterwork of educational excellence. Our broad overview begins with creating respectful relationships, moves through culturally responsive teaching, and culminates in a consistent evaluation of student engagement and achievement.

Now, we delve into the detailed steps, examining each strategy with the scrutiny of a master craftsman. Begin by establishing trust and respect within your classroom. It's the cornerstone of any learning environment—without it, the walls of potential crumble. Encourage open dialogue, learn the names and stories of your students, and show genuine interest in their lives. This is the thread that weaves a tapestry of trust.

126

Next, consider the curriculum through a lens of cultural responsiveness. Does it reflect the diversity of the students? Integrate literature, history, and perspectives that resonate with the black male experience. This not only validates their identity but also enriches the learning landscape for all students.

Transitioning into instruction, employ a variety of teaching methods to cater to different learning styles. From collaborative group work to technology-assisted learning, variety is the spice that can invigorate a classroom. Remember, a one-size-fits-all approach is the antithesis of inclusivity.

What about classroom management? Here, fairness and consistency are your allies. Develop clear, equitable rules and consequences and ensure they are applied without bias. It's a delicate balance, akin to a maestro conducting an orchestra—each note must be struck with precision to create harmony.

A word of practical advice: patience is your greatest virtue. Change rarely happens overnight. It's a gradual process, a journey marked by small victories and inevitable setbacks. And a caution: be wary of assumptions. Approach each student as an individual, a unique narrative unfolding before you.

How do we measure success? Look for increased participation, improved academic performance, and a palpable sense of belonging among your students. These are the signs that your strategies are taking root and blossoming.

Should you encounter resistance or relapse, do not despair. Troubleshooting is part of the process. Engage in reflective practice, seek feedback from colleagues, and be willing to adjust your approach. Flexibility is not a sign of weakness but of strength.

As you weave these strategies into the fabric of your daily teaching, you'll notice a transformation. It's the spark of confidence in a young man's eyes, the assertive raising of a hand, the eager sharing of ideas. This is the validation of your efforts, the proof that your classroom is becoming a crucible of empowerment.

Can you envision it? A classroom that is not merely a space but a sanctuary, a place where every student, regardless of color or background, can see their potential mirrored back at them.

As educators, your influence extends beyond the confines of the classroom. You are sculptors of the future, and with every inclusive practice you implement, you chisel away at the monolith of inequality.

CHANGE BEGINS WITH YOU.

Simple language, profound truth. Let this mantra echo through the halls and resonate in the classrooms. The rhythm of your dedication the cadence of your commitment, will set the tempo for a revolution in education.

Remember, your voice has power. "To teach is to touch a life forever," as the adage goes. May your touch be gentle yet transformative, guiding your students toward a horizon of limitless potential.

Strategies for Educators is more than a chapter; it's a manual for metamorphosis. It's an invitation to join hands and hearts in the noble pursuit of equality and excellence.

The journey is ongoing, the destination is clear, and together, we can reach it.

POLICY RECOMMENDATIONS

In the quest to dismantle barriers and pave pathways for black male student success, policy recommendations play a pivotal role. They are the blueprint for systemic change, the actionable steps that can transform educational landscapes. What follows is a focused exploration of these recommendations, each a thread in the fabric of a more equitable and just system.

The policies outlined here are not mere suggestions; they are urgent calls to action, each with the potential to significantly alter the trajectory of black male students' academic journeys. Let us delve into these transformative measures, understanding that their successful implementation could be the dawn of a new era in education.

1. Equitable Funding for Schools

2. Recruitment and Retention of Diverse Educators

3. Culturally Relevant Curriculum and Pedagogy

4. Comprehensive Student Support Systems

5. Enhanced Parental and Community Engagement

6. Standardized Test Reforms

7. School-to-Prison Pipeline Dismantlement

The stark disparities in funding between schools serving primarily black students and their counterparts is a chasm that continues to widen. Equitable funding must be more than a goal; it must be a mandate. This involves allocating resources based on student needs ensuring that all students, regardless of their zip code, have access to quality facilities, advanced technology, and enriching programs.

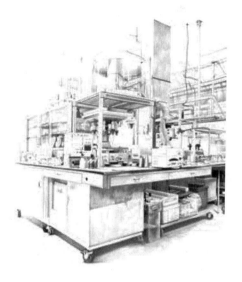

Studies repeatedly show that increased funding in low-income schools leads to improved student outcomes. According to research, a 10% increase in per-pupil spending each year for all 12 years of public school leads to 0.27 more completed years of education, higher wages, and a reduction in the incidence of adult poverty.

Imagine classrooms equipped with up-to-date textbooks, laboratories with the latest equipment, and libraries brimming with resources. These are not luxuries; they are essentials for learning that should be afforded to every student.

The presence of black male educators can have a profound impact on students, serving as role models and mentors. Recruiting educators from diverse backgrounds is crucial, but retention is equally important. This requires creating supportive environments that value their contributions and provide opportunities for professional growth.

Data indicates that having just one black teacher in elementary school reduces the probability of black students dropping out of high school by 29%. For very low-income black boys, the results are even more significant—a 39% reduction.

A school where the faculty mirrors the diversity of the student body is a school where every student can see themselves not only belonging but thriving in academic and professional realms.

Curriculum and teaching that acknowledge and celebrate the cultural backgrounds of students can validate their identities and enhance their educational engagement. This means incorporating the history, literature, and perspectives of black individuals and communities into the curriculum.

Research supports that culturally relevant teaching improves academic achievement, student motivation, and the classroom climate. When students see themselves represented in their studies, they are more likely to engage and excel.

Visualize a history lesson that not only covers the Civil Rights Movement but also delves into the contributions of black scientists, authors, and leaders throughout history—a lesson that is both reflective and aspirational for black male students.

Support systems that acknowledge the whole student— academic, emotional, social, and physical—are essential. This includes access to counselors, mentors, after-school programs, and health services that cater to the unique challenges faced by black male students.

A study by the American Psychological Association highlighted that access to school-based mental health services significantly improves educational outcomes for students, particularly those at risk of failing.

Consider a school that not only teaches math and science but also provides a safe space for students to discuss their challenges, hopes, and dreams, supported by professionals who understand and advocate for their well-being.

Parents and community members are invaluable allies in the educational process. Policies that encourage their participation through flexible meeting times, language translation services, and active roles in decision-making can strengthen the school-community bond.

Research has consistently shown that parental involvement is a strong predictor of student academic success. When parents are engaged, students receive higher grades and test scores, have better social skills, and are more likely to graduate.

Envision a school environment where parents are not just spectators but active participants, contributing their voices to the symphony of education and playing a key role in shaping the experiences of their children.

The reliance on standardized tests as the primary measure of student ability and school effectiveness is deeply flawed. Policies must move towards more holistic assessment methods that consider multiple facets of student learning and potential.

Experts argue that high-stakes testing can disproportionately disadvantage minority students, who may not have equal access to test preparation resources. Alternative assessment methods could provide a more accurate representation of student abilities.

Imagine an academic world where success is measured not by a single test score but by a portfolio of accomplishments showcasing a student's strengths, improvements, and unique talents.

The school-to-prison pipeline is a disturbing national trend wherein children are funneled out of public schools and into the juvenile and criminal justice systems. Policies must address this by reforming disciplinary practices and promoting restorative justice in schools.

Statistics show that black students are suspended and expelled at a rate three times greater than white students. These disciplinary actions often mark the beginning of a child's path into the criminal justice system.

Picture a school that replaces zero-tolerance policies with restorative practices, where conflicts are resolved through mediation and dialogue, fostering an environment of understanding and growth.

In weaving these recommendations into the educational tapestry, we create a portrait of possibility, a landscape where every black male student is afforded the dignity, respect, and opportunity he deserves. The question before us is not whether change is needed but whether we have the collective will to enact it. Are we prepared to transform these policies from words on a page into the lived reality of our students? The answer must be a resounding yes. For in the success of these young men lies the success of our society as a whole.

COMMUNITY ENGAGEMENT

In the heart of a bustling urban neighborhood, where the pulse of community life beats strong against the backdrop of history and tradition, a movement is taking root. It is here, among the murals depicting great leaders and the vibrant hum of local gatherings, that a powerful story unfolds—a story of determination, collaboration, and triumph in the face of adversity.

At the center of this narrative stand the main players: a local high school, a grassroots community organization, and a group of dedicated black male students. The high school, long-standing and rich in heritage, has faced its share of challenges, serving a student population grappling with the systemic inequities that too often dictate the educational landscape. The community organization, led by passionate advocates for social justice, operates on the frontline of change, determined to uplift the youth of the neighborhood. The students, each a mosaic of potential and resilience, are eager to carve their paths but are often hindered by obstacles invisible to many.

The challenge laid bare is multifaceted—a complex blend of social, economic, and institutional barriers that have historically undermined the success of black male students. Low expectations, scarce resources, and a lack of representation in the curriculum and staff have conspired to dim the bright light of possibility for these young minds.

In response to this entrenched challenge, the community organization initiated a bold approach: to forge a partnership with the school and create an ecosystem of support and empowerment for black male students. They launched mentoring programs, career workshops, and cultural events, all meticulously designed to integrate the richness of the students' heritage with the pursuit of academic excellence.

The strategies employed were as diverse as the community itself. Mentors from various professional backgrounds committed to regular sessions with students, providing guidance, encouragement, and exposure to new opportunities. Career workshops connected classroom learning with real-world applications, inspiring students to envision a future beyond the confines of their current circumstances. Cultural events celebrated the students' identities, fostering a sense of pride and belonging.

The results of this concerted effort were nothing short of transformative. Graduation rates began to climb, college acceptance letters flooded in, and the once-muted aspirations of these students now echoed loudly in the halls of achievement. Data collected over the course of the program showed marked improvements in academic performance, attendance, and student engagement.

Reflecting on the journey, it becomes clear that while the program's successes are worthy of celebration, they also prompt a critical analysis. How can this model be replicated and scaled to benefit more communities? What lessons can be extracted to inform broader strategies for change? The answers lie in the unwavering commitment to listen, adapt, and remain rooted in the needs and strengths of the community.

Visual aids, such as infographics depicting the program's impact on student outcomes or photographs capturing the vibrant cultural events, would further illustrate the profound influence of community engagement on student success.

This case study is not an isolated tale; it is a microcosm of the larger narrative that underscores the importance of community involvement in the educational journeys of black male students. It reaffirms the notion that when given the right support and opportunities, these students can not only succeed but soar.

As we turn the page on this chapter, let us ponder a question that propels us forward: What untapped potential lies within our communities, waiting to be ignited by the power of collective action? The answer is a beacon guiding our next steps, illuminating the path toward a future where every student, regardless of race or background, is granted the opportunity to achieve their fullest potential.

A VISION FOR THE FUTURE

Imagine a world where the narrative has shifted, where the success of black male students is not an exception but a widespread reality. This is not a distant dream but a future within our grasp—a promise I make to you as we embark on this transformative journey through the pages of "Shattered Reflections: Unraveling the Hidden Journey of Black Male Student Success."

Somewhere in the not-so-distant future, classrooms echo with the robust exchange of ideas, halls are lined with the portraits of black scholars, and success stories are as common as the sunrise. But how do we construct this future? Within this book lies a blueprint, a series of actionable steps grounded in rigorous research and the lived experiences of those who have walked this path before.

I know what you're thinking—can one book really make such a difference? It's a fair question. Skepticism often arises when promises of change are made, particularly in a landscape riddled with false starts and unmet expectations. Yet here, I offer you not just empty assurances but a repository of tested strategies and unvarnished truths drawn from the well of my experience as a scholar and advocate for change.

Envision with me, for a moment, the transformation that awaits. See the young black student, head full of dreams and a heart full of ambition, stepping onto the stage to receive his diploma, his gaze set firmly on the horizon of his future. Picture the educator, eyes alight with pride, who has watched that student overcome and rise, knowing that the fight for equity has found another champion.

This vision is not a mere fantasy; it is a destiny that can be sealed with commitment and guided by the insights shared in these pages. The value of this journey is beyond measure, for it is one that reshapes lives, rewrites stories, and reclaims futures that were once obscured by the shadows of doubt and discrimination.

Dive deep into the heart of this book, and you will uncover strategies that defy tradition—innovative mentoring programs that connect students with leaders who mirror their potential, curricula that honor and reflect the rich tapestry of black history and policies that dismantle barriers to educational access and excellence. Picture an academic environment where black male students are not only surviving but thriving, their achievements a testament to their resilience and the effectiveness of the methodologies laid out before you.

What if the key to unlocking this future was in recognizing the unique strengths that black male students bring to the table? What if the transformation required a collective effort, one that calls on educators, policymakers, and community leaders to forge a new alliance for change?

Can you feel the groundswell of a revolution in education, where each success story adds a verse to an ever-growing anthem of empowerment? This is not a solitary fight; it is a chorus that rises when voices join in unity, echoing the promise of equity and excellence for all.

You might wonder, is this vision too idealistic, too removed from the gritty realities of the present day? Let me assure you, this is not a call to gaze upon the world through rose-tinted glasses. It is, instead, an invitation to confront the challenges head-on, armed with the knowledge and strategies that have been tried, tested, and proven to make a difference.

It's time to ask ourselves: What role will we play in this unfolding story? How will we contribute to the reclamation of hope and the nurturing of greatness that resides within each student?

As you delve further into these pages, you will encounter tales of triumph, strategies for success, and a clarion call to action that resonates with urgency and purpose. This book is more than a mere collection of words; it is a catalyst for a revolution that begins in the heart of education and ripples outward, touching every facet of society.

Allow me to leave you with this final thought: the journey we are on is not just about changing the trajectory of black male students—it's about transforming the very fabric of our educational system, ensuring that every student, regardless of race or background, is valued, supported, and given the opportunity to excel.

This is our vision for the future. This is the legacy we can build together. Let the pages that follow serve as your guide, your inspiration, and your unwavering companion as we step boldly into a brighter, more equitable tomorrow.